GW00468034

FURTHER WEIRD CASES

Comic and bizarre cases from courtrooms around the world

Gary Slapper

Wildy, Simmonds & Hill Publishing

Slapper, G J

Further Weird Cases: Comic and bizarre cases from courtrooms around the world

ISBN 9780854901340

Printed and bound in Great Britain

PREFACE

A cross the world, law courts hear some of the most extraordinary and bizarre examples of human drama that it is possible to imagine.

The first book in this series, *Weird Cases*, was published in 2010 and contained cases which had been dealt with by the courts in the previous two years. The second book, *More Weird Cases*, was published in 2012. The parade of legal cases featuring periodically astonishing human disputes and irregularities has naturally run on unabated since then. It will run for as long as our species inhabits the earth.

Courtroom drama is tense, compelling and mostly very serious. By virtue of having ended up in court, all civil, family and criminal disputes involve human beings in fraught situations. Mundane behaviour does not, by definition, get taken to court. The cases featured in this book are those that stand out as odd even among all the unusual dramas that challenge the courts.

The cases include that of a man from Florida who, after he had his hand bitten off by a reptile, was convicted of "illegally feeding an alligator"; a case from Pennsylvania in which a man sued the Inland Revenue Service for keeping him on tenterhooks for 24 years about whether his job application was successful; and a case about whether a public servant from Canberra, who was injured while she was having sex with a friend in a motel room during a work trip, was entitled to workplace compensation.

Other cases in the chapters feature a Brazilian election candidate who tried to gain votes by including a free sample of cocaine with each election leaflet; the question of whether a snack product called "Nuckin Futs" was too rude to register in Australia; a man from Ohio whom the courts refused to declare alive because he had been judicially declared dead over three years earlier; and the defendant who urinated in the judge's waste paper bin.

As in the earlier books in this series, the cases are organised in themed chapters related to topics such as punishment and compensation, love and sex, food, drink and drugs, children and animals, and technology.

This book arises from a weekly column called *Weird Cases* which I write for *The Times* online. The cases here were first covered there.

I have aimed to keep the text as free as possible of technical legal words and phrases.

ACKNOWLEDGEMENTS

I am deeply indebted to my family – Suzanne, Hannah, Emily, and Charlotte – for their enduring support.

My original interest in weird legal cases was developed when I noticed at family dinner table discussions that these stories drew much more interest than long perorations on corporate law.

I am very grateful to Martha Spurrier at Doughty Street Chambers for her superb work in assisting with the arrangement of the cases. I am also grateful for the professionalism, encouragement and wry humour of Frances Gibb, Legal Editor at The Times, and to Sandra White, Assistant Editor for Law.

I am much indebted to Andrew Riddoch, Commissioning Editor at Wildy, Simmonds & Hill, for his continuing support and encouragement.

Many others have aided and abetted this venture in various ways. I thank my parents Doreen and Ivor Slapper – the books were my father's idea. I thank Clifford, Maxine, Pav, Anish, the late Raie Schwartz, David and Julie Whight, Hugh McLaughlan, Abigail Carr, Carolyn Bracknell, Lulu Phillips, Dr Anoop Nayar, HH Judge Lynn Tayton QC, Sheriff Andrew M Cubie, Carol Howells, the late Jane Goodey, Ken Shaw, Patrick Whight, Malcolm Park, and Dr David Kelly.

By the same author

Weird Cases

More Weird Cases

CONTENTS

Chapter 1

Punishment and Compensation

Worldwide, law libraries the size of warehouses brim with volumes on the rules of punishment and compensation. These themes are at the core of law.

Criminal cases are generally brought by the state for conduct ranging from graffiti to murder. If the defendant is found guilty, punishment will follow. The English jurist, Herbert Hart, wrote that at the core of our legal system we need rules against violence to stop society becoming a "suicide club". Most legal systems began from rules of elemental importance such as "thou shalt not kill". Today, there are thousands of rules controlling every conceivable type of violence, including threats and emotional assault.

The law is now framed to cover a massively diverse range of wrongdoing. There are over 12,000 offences under English law. Between 1997 and 2009, 4,289 separate offences were the subject of legislation. These include disturbing a pack of eggs when directed not to do so by an authorised officer, selling or offering for sale game birds which have been shot on a Sunday, and swimming in the wreck of the Titanic.

Civil cases are brought by citizens or organisations and the aim is usually to get compensation or a court order to make someone do something or stop doing something. Although the number of cases being heard in civil courts is not rising dramatically in many jurisdictions, there is evidence of a growth in "compensation culture" and the propensity of people to commence litigation.

The chapter on this theme in the previous book in the series, *More Weird Cases*, included cases in which an aristocrat claimed his human rights had been violated with the cruel and unusual punishment of having to wear ill-fitting underpants in prison, a man who tried to sue the *Guinness Book of World Records* for calling him the world's most litigious man, a man who was convicted for claiming unemployment benefits when he was actually working at an employment office, and a restaurant worker who gained compensation after his fist was injured punching a customer. There follows another catalogue of oddities from the world of punishment and compensation.

Rack and ruin

Saint Augustine observed that "punishment is justice for the unjust". Some convicted people, however, get more justice than others. In Waco, Texas in 2013, a man convicted of stealing a rack of ribs was sent to prison for 50 years.

Willie Smith Ward was convicted and sentenced on robbery charges. His theft of the US$35 rack of pork ribs from a grocery turned into the more serious charge of robbery (theft with violence or the threat of violence) after he told a store employee who tried to stop him that he had a knife. Mr Ward tried to pilfer the ribs from the store by concealing them under his shirt. The employee testified that he asked Mr Ward what was under the shirt and the slab of meat fell to the ground. He then asked Mr Ward what else he was hiding and Ward said "I got a knife". The employee said that he then told Mr Ward "Now you just turned a ticket into a serious crime". According to the employee, Mr Ward replied "If you don't leave me alone, I'll show you what I got" and then he ran off. The event was in 2011 but the sentence was confirmed, after a long legal process, in 2013. At one point, Mr Ward was offered a 20-year prison sentence in return for a guilty plea but he rejected it. His sentence was stringent as he had a list of previous convictions. The jury in Waco's 19th State District Court recommended Mr Ward be sentenced as an "habitual criminal". Mr Ward had previous felony convictions for burglary, attempted robbery, aggravated assault, leaving the scene of an accident, and possession of cocaine.

A sentence of 50 years is severe but is significantly shorter than some of history's most punitive incarcerations. The longest recorded prison sentence for a crime is one of 43,000 years. Two people from Morocco and one from Spain were each given that sentence for the bombing of four commuter trains at Madrid station in 2004.

A sentence of 6,616 years, six months and one day was imposed on José Ruiz by a court in Madrid, on 19 April 1967. The sentence comprised consecutive terms for the sale of each of many non-existent holiday flats on the Costa Brava. It is not stated in the court report whether Mr Ruiz would become eligible for parole after serving half his sentence.

The softest sentence meted out by a court was that given to Joan Meredith by the Bench at Alnwick Magistrates' Court in Northumberland in 2000. She was punished under section 135 of the Magistrates' Court Act 1980 which permitted a detention "within the precincts of the court-house ... until such hour, not later than 8 o'clock in the evening of the day on which the order is made, as the court may direct". Ms Meredith, a 70-year-old anti-nuclear protester from Rock Moor, was excused a £100 fine and the alternative of a week in prison for her part in a peace protest at Faslane naval base. Instead, she was ordered to find a comfortable seat in the court and stay there for the rest of the day.

Please Mr Postman, is there a letter for me?

Paul Chulhie Kim isn't the first American to blame the Internal Revenue Service (IRS) for his problems. His complaint, however, heard by a court in Pennsylvania in 2013, is one of the most unusual.

Mr Kim claimed he had suffered 24 years of ill-health because the IRS never got back to him following his attendance at a job open day at a tax office in "approximately 1989". Certainly, that is a long time to be waiting anxiously at his letter box for a reply. The case was heard by US District Judge Edmund V Ludwig, sitting in the Eastern District of Pennsylvania. Mr Kim argued that he was told that to be hired as a computer data entry clerk he would need to take a federal examination. He was told, he said, that the IRS would choose applicants with the highest scores, and that as a federal employer it would give preference to military veterans. Mr Kim was a military veteran and scored full marks in the exam, but he claimed he was never given a job interview. In a lawsuit filed without a lawyer in January 2013, Mr Kim alleged that he had been "waiting 24 years now" and that as a result of this long-term unemployment, he had suffered serious health problems, such as "starvation, heart attacks, heart failure, kidney failure, liver failure, pneumonia, seizures, cancer [and] mental illness".

Mr Kim alleged "employment discrimination by a federal agency". Normally, legal actions begun years after an incident are barred by a law known as "a statute of limitations". In this case, Mr Kim recognised the applicability of that law (in his claim he said he had been a "Harvard scholar") but asked the court to lift the statute of limitations because, among other things, the attorneys he had consulted years ago would not take his case. He blamed his failure to start the action nearer its occurrence on bad lawyers. In this case, Mr Kim claimed US$20 million in damages to restore his "trust in the American people" and to restore confidence in his US citizenship. In dismissing the case, Judge Ludwig ruled that the employment discrimination action was flawed in several ways. It did not, for example, specify the basis upon which the claimant believed the IRS discriminated against him.

Occasionally, cases take an extraordinarily long time to resolve, even after they get to court. The judgment of one decision of the Court of Appeal in Britain begins "It is 12 years since this discrimination dispute began. It arose out of two unsuccessful job applications at the end of the 20th century. The case is now a 21st-century version of a 19th-century Chancery saga. And it is not over yet". The "19th-century Chancery saga" referred to was the case that inspired Charles Dickens to write in *Bleak House* about the fictitious case of *Jarndyce v Jarndyce*. The case was about an inheritance dispute wrangled over in court for so many generations that legal costs eventually gobbled up the entire estate. The fictional case is almost certainly based on the real case of *Jennens v Jennens* which began in 1798 and had been going on for 55 years when *Bleak House* was published. The case, however, continued after Dickens' death in 1870 and was not abandoned until 1915 – 117 years after it began – when the legal fees had eaten away the entire Jennens estate. Describing Jarndyce, Dickens wrote "Innumerable children have been born into the cause ... [t]he little plaintiff or defendant, who was promised a new rocking horse when *Jarndyce v Jarndyce* should be settled, has grown up, possessed himself of a real horse, and trotted away into the other world."

Love on a small scale

In 2012, a Dutch case broke new ground when an ant took centre stage.

In the Netherlands, the High Court heard the appeal of a homeless man who had been convicted of a criminal offence by calling a police officer a *mierenneuker* – an ant-fucker. The word *mierenneuker* is used in popular speech to refer to someone who sticks obsessively to the rules in the smallest way. The case began in 2010 when the man, identified in the law report as Sietze J, called a policeman a *mierenneuker* for throwing away his can of beer. The defendant was found guilty by a lower court which ruled Mr J had insulted the police officer. The case then went to the High Court on appeal. The court ruled that the precise legal meaning of *mierenneuker* depends on the context in which it is used. In some contexts, it can be construed as offensive swearing but not in all contexts. Only if *mierenneuker* is used with the intention to insult or cause offence is it a swear word, the High Court ruled. Coskun Çörüz, a Dutch MP who commented on the case, said "If you can call a police officer, one of the mainstays of the rule of law, an ant-fucker, then it worries me what you can call a teacher, a prison warder, a traffic warden or a social benefits officer."

Before the ant insult, previous Dutch decisions in cases of alleged insults to police officers have been dealt with very strictly. In 2010, three men were fined €330 each for wearing t-shirts with the numbers 1312 printed on them, which stands in number-letter code for ACAB, which is said to mean "All Cops Are Bastards".

In 1977, in Connecticut, Justice Parskey ruled that a school boy who had "given the finger" (a closed-fist manual gesture with an extended middle finger) from the rear window of a bus to a state trooper was not guilty of making an "obscene gesture". The court held that, as used by Diogenes as a "semiotic insult" to the orator Demosthenes, the *digitus impudicus* (the impudent finger), or *katapugon* in Greek, was a phallic symbol, but both then and when directed at a police officer in America, it was calculated to arouse anger rather than sexual desire, so was not obscene.

A court in New Zealand, however, developed the most unusual order in a case of an insult directed against police officers. After he drove slowly past police in Western Bay in 2005, and called the officers "pig shit", a 22-year-old man was ordered by Tauranga District Court to spend a day on a pig farm wading about in pig material, and then write an essay for the court to make it clear he comprehended the difference between the farm animals and the local constabulary.

A step too far

A case in Illinois from 2012 set a curious precedent as compensation was awarded to a state worker whose harm resulted from "repetitive walking".

In *Howell v State of Illinois and Menard Correctional Centre*, Tracy Howell won over US$70,000 compensation for injury to his Achilles tendon which was related, he said, to the several miles a day he had to walk across, up and down prison tiers. The arbitrator found that Mr Howell had suffered "repetitive/cumulative trauma" as the result of his work and had suffered significantly through the "stress" of walking several miles a day.

An American news organisation, Belleville News-Democrat, reviewed cases and found that in recent times, the Menard Correctional Centre, a high-security prison, was the source of 230 repetitive trauma claims resulting in settlement payments in excess of US$10 million. Most of the claims were from guards who were claiming compensation for hands and elbows injured by turning keys and using locking systems.

Eugene Keefe, an American lawyer and academic, has observed that legal policy which allows compensation for "repetitive walking" might not be good for American health. He cited a study published in 2003 which tracked the steps of 1,136 adults around the United States who wore pedometers for two days. The data collected showed that Americans, on average, took 5,117 steps a day, significantly fewer than the averages in western Australia (9,695 steps), Switzerland (9,650 steps) and Japan (7,168 steps). Permitting "repetitive walking" litigation would be likely to widen the gap.

It is an open question whether the Illinois Workers' Compensation Commission, which confirmed the award in the "repetitive walking" case, will be bound to make similar awards in cases where applicants claim ill-health or injury from "repetitive reading" or "repetitive sitting". It would, arguably, also be open to advocates to sue the court system for ill-health consequent upon "repetitive standing" after many years on their feet in courtrooms.

The American litigation system has seen some unusual personal injury cases. Richard Overton from Michigan sued Anheuser-Busch, the manufacturers of Budweiser, for US$10,000 for its beer adverts. He claimed to have suffered much harm including emotional distress and mental injury due to "misleading" Bud Light adverts. One particular objection of his was the television advert for Bud Light involving two men, a beer truck and fantasies of "tropical settings, beautiful women and men engaged in endless and unrestricted merriment". He complained the advert promoted "impossible manifestations". In 1994, the Michigan Court of Appeals ruled that the fantasies represented in such adverts are not expected to stand up to the rational analysis of the courtroom. Mr Overton's claim was very soberly rejected by the judges.

In 2004, Timothy Dumouchel, from Fond du Lac, Wisconsin sued a television company for making his wife obese and transforming his children into "lazy channel surfers". He said "I believe the reason I smoke and drink every day and my wife is overweight is because we watched the TV every day for the last four years". He claimed that he asked the company Charter Communication to disconnect his service four years earlier. He was removed from its billing system but the service wasn't stopped so it was delivered free. This kept at least two of America's then 1,058,662 lawyers occupied for a while, but the case did not go to the Supreme Court.

The fountain of injustice

Justice must flow from a revered source. In the UK, for example, the monarch is constitutionally known as "the fountain of justice and mercy". Not all fountains, however, are associated with justice and mercy.

After a hungry, penniless, mentally disabled woman in Ohio took US$2.87 (£1.77) in coins from a public fountain, she was charged with theft and made to face a jail term. In 2013, Deidre Romine was walking by the Logan County Courthouse in Bellefontaine (which happens to mean beautiful fountain) when she scooped some coins from a public fountain. She did not think the money belonged to anyone in particular, and explained to the police officer who apprehended her that she took it because she was hungry and needed food. Judged by what happened next, the place called Bellefontaine might have momentarily lapsed into a town better titled as the Unforgiving Fountain. To deter any other mentally disabled, hungry citizens from scraping coins from the fountain, Ms Romine was charged with petty theft of US$2.87 and made to face the prospect of up to 180 days in jail. Citizens at large took a more compassionate view than the justice system of her plight. An internet fund for her benefit gained US$6,000 within a week of being established.

There is a legal principle known as *de minimis non curat lex* – the law takes no account of trifling matters. Trying a case of burglary worth 40 shillings at the Old Bailey in the 18th century when that was the threshold of a capital offence, Lord Mansfield was horrified that a man should be hanged for taking one golden trinket, so he asked the jury to value it at under 40 shillings. When the prosecutor objected, saying even the fashion alone of the trinket was worth over 40 shillings, Lord Mansfield replied "God forbid, gentlemen, we should hang a man for fashion's sake!"

In a case in 1820, Mr Justice Scott said that "irregularities of very slight consequence" which there is little or no purpose in punishing "might properly be overlooked" by prosecuting authorities. That principle, however, was not applied in the case of Ms Romine.

Other evidently trifling matters have also occupied the law. In England in 2006, David, an 11-year-old from Doncaster, was fined £50 for accidentally dropping an apple core outside his school. The apple had fallen from the shallow pocket of this well-behaved boy, and he had apologised to the litter warden who spotted the event. A spokeswoman for the authority which fined him said "there are no exemptions from the zero tolerance campaign".

The yawning jaws of justice

In court, people must exhibit just the right degree of interest – you're not allowed to show any sign of being either bored or entertained. In Scotland in 2012, a man was prosecuted for yawning in court, while in North Carolina another man landed himself in trouble for laughing in court.

At Alloa Sheriff Court, near Stirling in Scotland, Thomas Tams faced a single charge that he conducted himself in a disorderly manner and committed a breach of the peace by "yawning loudly whilst the court was sitting". Mr Tams, 35, pleaded not guilty. In addition to showing signs of tiredness, Mr Tams, of Alva, Clackmannanshire, was said to have refused to comply with an instruction from the clerk of court about his conduct in the courtroom.

Yawning in court has seldom been penalised anywhere in the world, although there is one severe sentencing precedent. In a serious criminal case in Walasmulla, Sri Lanka in 2004, the defendant emitted a weary yawn at the beginning of the proceedings against him. Judge AKM Patabendige instantly suspended the assault case and jailed him for contempt for a year.

No matter how tedious a case gets, courtroom boredom should never be made manifest. Lord Birkett once noted "I do not object to people looking at their watches when I am speaking. But I strongly object when they start shaking them to make certain they are still going."

While being prosecuted for a drugs offence at St Albans Crown Court in 2006, Paul Phillips gave the impression he wasn't overly awed by his trial when he drifted well beyond a yawn and fell fast asleep in court. He was given a judicial alarm call and allowed a short adjournment because, the judge noted, it was "important for him to be aware of how his own trial was going".

Laughter in court is also forbidden. In North Carolina, a Cumberland County Judge took a dim view of a man who kept laughing in her court. Judge Toni King asked Johnny Montgomery, 47, what he found so amusing. In an unusual response to a judge in court, Mr Montgomery reportedly replied "It's none of your business". Judge King ordered him to be removed from her courtroom. Then, as officers searched Montgomery, they found more than three grams of crack cocaine on him. Montgomery was originally in court on misdemeanour charges of communicating threats and trespassing when laughter overcame him. He was then additionally charged with felony possession of cocaine.

Since the 13th century, English law has punished people who commit contempt "in the face of the court". Explaining the crime, Lord Denning noted that the course of justice must not be "deflected or interfered with" and that "those who strike at it strike at the very foundations of our society".

Laughing is a noted type of contempt of court. As the 20th-century American writer, Henry Louis Mencken, dryly noted, "the penalty for laughing in the courtroom is six months in jail: if it were not for this penalty, the jury would never hear the evidence".

The devil is in the detail

The Antichrist does not feature much in the case law of West Virginia. He did, however, make an appearance in an unusual employment law case in 2013.

In 2012, a biometric hand-scan system for monitoring the hours worked by its employees was installed at the Robinson Run mine in Mannington, West Virginia. The US Equal Employment Opportunity Commission (EEOC) later sued the company (Consol Inc. and its subsidiary Consolidated Coal which operates the mine) for having failed to provide an alternative system for Beverly Butcher, an employee, who refused to scan his hand because he said the scan was associated with the Mark of the Beast. Mr Butcher reported that he is an Evangelical Christian and believes he is not permitted to submit a hand for scanning. He refers to Book of Revelation (13:15–18) which says "The second beast ... forced all people, great and small, rich and poor, free and slave, to receive a mark on their right hands or on their foreheads ... which is the name of the beast or the number of its name". The passage goes on to say "Let he who has understanding count the number of the beast: for it is the number of a man; and his number is six hundred threescore and six".

Mr Butcher said he wrote to the company in 2012 expressing his genuinely held religious beliefs about the relationship between hand scanning and the Antichrist, and requested exemption from the practice. Recognition Systems Inc., the producer of the scanning equipment, then wrote to Mr Butcher discussing its interpretation of Revelation. It noted that the biblical verse refers only to "the right hand and forehead". Mr Butcher could, therefore, it suggested, use his left hand for the scanning. Mr Butcher, however, declined to accept that suggestion and resigned. The EEOC filed a suit for him in the US District

Court, saying that by declining to make a reasonable accommodation for his genuinely held religious belief, the defendants created working conditions "sufficiently intolerable that a reasonable person would feel compelled to end their employment".

The Antichrist has appeared in other cases. In 2009, the European Court of Human Rights rejected the claim of three Russian citizens who tried to get their tax numbers altered from sequences which contained a "666" element. They asserted their numbers were "the mark of the Antichrist" and that this violated their right to freedom of religious belief. The court rejected that argument, saying the method of assigning numbers to taxpayers did not amount to an interference with the applicants' right to freedom of religion.

Copping more than he bargained for

"Care and diligence bring luck", observed Thomas Fuller in London in 1732. In Indiana in 2012, Chadwyck Voegeli demonstrated that the opposite can also be true: recklessness can bring bad luck.

Mr Voegeli faced trial for impersonating a public servant. He was indicted after posing as a police officer in his car and using flashing lights to pull over a vehicle. It was bad luck for him, however, that the men whom he pulled over were police officers in an ordinary car. Mr Voegeli, 20, of Fort Wayne, had used an adapted mobile phone – flashing red and blue lights – to pull over the car as he drove down a main road. After he pulled alongside his intended victims, and the officers identified themselves, Voegeli allegedly sped off, ditched his car and ran through a bar before eventually being apprehended. He faced a felony charge of impersonation of a public servant and a misdemeanour charge of resisting law enforcement.

Occasionally, others impersonating police officers have encountered similar difficulties.

In 2010 in Detroit, a police officer in a car cruised slowly up to a prostitute at the roadside, flashed his police badge and shouted "get off the street". But things were not as they seemed. The police officer was really a criminal and the prostitute was really a police officer.

A female officer dressed as a sex worker was on the street about 5pm and was talking to a potential client – actually, a potential convict as he was in her eyes. Then William Quirindango drove up, identified himself as a police officer and challenged the prostitute. Hearing that, her prospective client ran away very fast. "Officer" Quirindango continued to hassle the prostitute, repeatedly barking at her the news that he was a police officer. The prostitute then revealed that she was in fact a police detective on an undercover operation, at which point Quirindango evidently remembered some other urgent cop business he had to attend to and sped off. Quirindango was not far into his next phantom mission, however, when he was caught by real officers. He denied he had done anything wrong but the police found in his car a Detroit Police Department (DPD) badge, items of police uniform including hats with DPD logos, and a loaded .40-calibre Glock handgun.

The legal theatre of the absurd has, however, one precedent of unsurpassable confusion. On the office wall of the late broadcaster and oral historian, Studs Terkel, was an enlarged and framed clipping taken from a Bangkok newspaper report from the early 1970s. It recorded a battle between police and a gang of bandits in southern Thailand in which a man was killed.

In the news report a police spokesman is quoted as saying that the deadly battle began "when the bandit gang, disguised as policemen, challenged a group of policemen, disguised as bandits".

Hot tickets

No football player has ever been dismissed for scoring too many goals. In an odd case from Palm Beach, Florida in 2012, however, a police officer was dismissed for issuing too many tickets to speeding motorists.

In a letter of termination, the Palm Beach director of public safety said that officer William Eaton had been guilty of "conduct unbecoming" and using his position to intimidate the citizenry when he wrote 115 traffic tickets in a 16-day period at the beginning of the year. After drivers complained of being persecuted, there was a suspicion that officer Eaton had acted in the way he did in protest at a council decision to alter police pension rights. The local director of public safety, Kirk Blouin, ordered an internal investigation and it reported that Eaton wrote 115 citations in the month following the town council's vote on 18 January 2012 approving major cuts in police pension benefits. By comparison, from 19 January 2011 to 18 February 2011, Eaton wrote only 16 traffic citations. From 18 December 2011 to 18 January 2012, Eaton wrote 25 citations. It was also alleged that Eaton, a member of the police force for six years, encouraged other officers to increase their citations, while boasting about his own prolific ticket-writing. Elizabeth Parker, officer Eaton's attorney, said that Mr Eaton started writing more tickets to more effectively perform his duties after the town changed its rules in January to give bonuses based on merit instead of longevity. The director of public safety, Mr Blouin, said that the previous year, in discussing the possible changes the council might make to pension rules, officer Eaton had made a threat. Mr Blouin alleged that officer Eaton had indicated that if the Palm Beach council – representative of local citizens – were to endorse cuts to the police pension, there might be retaliation against local citizens in the form of enforcing the law with a disturbing zeal. Mr Eaton flatly denied that he ever made such a threat.

Zealous policing has not been seen as legally problematic in England. In 2009, Sergeant Ali Livingstone, from Ipswich in Suffolk, became the officer with the most annual arrests in history. He had arrested 524 people in 12 months, an average of 2.2 arrests every working day. He said the key to arresting people was simply getting to work early and getting out of the office. "I start most shifts an hour or so before I commence duty", he declared, "This gives me a chance to research crimes and outstanding offenders."

Sometimes judges too have gone about their work with a startling zeal. Dealing with a West Country rebellion in

1685, Lord Chief Justice Jeffreys sentenced 300 people to death, and over 800 to be transported. He gave the death sentence to 114 people over just two days. The public didn't like what the judge did but the king approved.

Judges have also been occasionally overactive when asking questions in court. In overruling a conviction in a case in 1944 in which two prostitutes were accused of stealing from a client's wallet, the Court of Appeal noted it was wrong for the judge to have asked witnesses 495 questions.

Not saved by the bell

In China, the *gaokao*, a manically competitive university entrance exam, is treated with great seriousness. Police road-blocks are set up around exam centres, and nearby construction sites are ordered to stop work and remain silent for the duration of the exam. A teacher in the province of Hunan in 2012 was sentenced to a year in prison for ringing the bell to end the exam five minutes early in one year's exam.

Xiao Yulong, 54, admitted having rung the bell at the school four minutes and 48 seconds early "by mistake". Consequently, 1,050 students had to hand in their exam scripts before they were required to do so. Over nine million students take the exam annually but only about one in 50 gets a university place and thus the chance, in most cases, of pulling their family from poverty. The incident, therefore, caused thousands of students and parents to gather at both the school and the local education bureau to demand that the government investigate. A prosecution followed. A court found that the invigilator, Mr Xiao, was careless in his work and mistakenly rang the bell too early, resulting in an "adverse social impact". Xiao was sentenced to one year in jail for criminal negligence. He was, however, given an order of clemency so he will not serve his full sentence.

There are some odd precedents of severe legal intervention in the educational process in other jurisdictions. In 2010, for example, Alexa Gonzalez, a 12-year-old girl from Queens in New York, was handcuffed by police and hauled away from her classroom after being reported for doodling on a desk in an erasable marker.

Outside the area of education, law courts have sometimes reacted extraordinarily where timing in the courtroom has been imperfect by a few minutes.

In 2011, the Honourable Justice Howard Chisvin in Ontario, Canada displayed a loss of temper when a prosecutor was three minutes late after a recess. The judge became so upset, he dismissed 12 serious criminal cases which the prosecutor was going to address, including robbery, fraud, crime committed by a psychiatric offender, and domestic abuse. On the day in question, at 11:23:11 the judge called for a 20-minute break. Although he had returned late himself by two minutes (11:45:21) he then went into meltdown when he saw the crown prosecutor, Bruce McCallion, wasn't yet back in court. The judge waited for a further two minutes, then, at 11.47, less than four minutes after the end of the recess, he snapped "All right, all provincial matters are dismissed for want of prosecution". He set free 12 defendants all of whom had already pleaded guilty or were intending to do so. The freed guilty people included violent offenders and a disbarred lawyer with one previous conviction for a US$1.2m fraud against clients.

Driving sign

A notable sentence of Judge Pinkey S Carr in Cleveland, Ohio, was not designed primarily to rehabilitate the convict.

For repeatedly driving on the sidewalk around a school bus while children were boarding in 2012, Shena Hardin, 32, was ordered to wear a placard in public identifying herself as an idiot. Hardin would routinely drive on the sidewalk to go around a school bus while children were getting on it. The bus driver alerted police who then waited one morning and caught her in the act. As her punishment, Judge Carr ordered her to stand at a nearby road intersection wearing a sign for two days reading "ONLY AN IDIOT DRIVES ON THE SIDEWALK

TO AVOID A SCHOOL BUS". She was ordered to wear the sign between 7:45am and 8:45am on both days. Her driving licence was suspended for 30 days and she was ordered to pay US$250 in court costs.

The use of shaming punishments like the stocks and pillories was historically common in Europe and existed in the United States before modern model criminal codes. But some forms of humiliating sentence have become more common in recent times.

In 2003, in Texas, Judge Buddie Hahn gave an abusive father a choice between spending 30 nights in jail or 30 nights sleeping in the doghouse where prosecutors alleged the man had forced his 11-year-old stepson to sleep. The father opted for the 3-foot by 2-foot doghouse.

In Georgia in 2011, Judge Sidney Nation suspended almost all of a seven-year sentence for cocaine possession and driving under the influence in exchange for the defendant's sworn undertaking to purchase a casket and keep it in his home to remind him of the costs of drug addiction.

In 2012, Utah District Juvenile Judge Scott Johansen gave a mother of a teenager who had cut off the long hair of a toddler the choice of either cutting off the ponytail of her miscreant daughter in open court or accepting a longer sentence for the teenager. The judge gave the mother, Valerie Bruno, a pair of scissors and she conceded, cutting off the pony tail of her 13-year-old daughter, right up to the rubber band.

For a noise nuisance offence involving rap music played from a car, Michael Carreras was sentenced by a court in Florida in 2004 to listen to Verdi's *La Traviata*. Judge Jeffrey Swartz, of Miami Beach, said "You impose your music on me, and I'm going to impose my music on you". Carreras, who was convicted of blasting rapper 50 Cent out of his car radio at 5am, was given the option of paying a US$500 fine or going into the judge's chambers to listen to Verdi for two and a half hours.

The convict experiencing the greatest relief for getting an unusual sentence option was 28-year-old Alparslan Yigit in 2003. He was convicted of being drunk and disorderly in public and accepted the punishment of attending a library and reading books for 90 minutes every day for a month. The alternative would have been 15 days in a Turkish prison.

A new world order

In 2013, the criminal justice system in Racine, Wisconsin made an order applying across the whole world.

Tyree Carter faced charges of lewd and lascivious behaviour, and disorderly conduct in the town's public library. He was accused of openly committing a solo sexual act in the library and faced imprisonment and fines of up to US$11,000. He was granted bail on a bond of US$1000 but a court order was attached banning Mr Carter from entering "all libraries on the face of the earth". There are over 300,000 public libraries in the world and Mr Carter would have been in breach of the order if he entered any of them. A library employee alleged that when she saw Mr Carter *in flagrante delicto*, he was on the second floor, "standing in the open, not trying to conceal the act". Police were summoned and when an officer approached him later, Mr Carter was sitting at a table reading a book. Mr Carter initially denied that he knew why the police had been called. When, however, an officer explained the complaint, Mr Carter allegedly apologised for his conduct and said he had not behaved in that way in public on any previous occasion.

Orders applying to the whole world are not unknown. In 2011, the High Court in London issued a *contra mundum* order – a worldwide ban – in the case of a man who wanted to stop publication of material about his private life. Such an order controls the conduct of a person or company within the theoretical jurisdiction of a court, wherever they go in the world.

Other odd cases have arisen in libraries. In 1961, analysing the criminal law, Lord Justice Devlin distinguished "real crimes" from lesser wrongs. Culprits of lesser wrongs, he noted "should not be treated with any more ignominy than a man who has incurred a penalty for failing to return a library book in time". That distinction was applied in a library case in New Zealand in 2006.

Marie Sushames returned *The Punch Library of Humour* to the Rotorua public library, and apologised as it was overdue. Overdue by 61 years. The fine was calculated at £3,500 but, on the Devlin principle, was remitted.

In 2003, Mr B Ranganathan, a politician in India, was charged with intimidation in connection with a land deal. He was given a bail order by Justice Vinayagam of the Madras High Court, with the condition that he spent four days in a library reading Gandhi. The judge said it was to make him "realise his duties" as a legislator. The defendant edified himself by turning over many new leaves in Gandhi's autobiography, *The Story of My Experiments with Truth.*

Chapter 2

Love and Sex

Legal cases often reveal major differences among people about the nature of relationships. The themes of love and sex have triggered contentious opinions from some quarters. Lord Chesterfield, the 18th-century statesman, for example, might have been revealing too much of his personal life when he said of sex that it was objectionable because "the pleasure is momentary, the position is ridiculous, and the expense damnable". Roseanne Barr was equally sceptical in a different way in suggesting that "all human beings connect sex and love – except for men".

Love and sex are exquisitely ill-suited to being dissected and scrutinised in the emotionally cold and judgmental forum of a law court. When they *are* subject to the attentions of lawyers and judges, the analytical exercise takes on a preposterousness that few formal dramas can match.

Love is a wild and multi-coloured pursuit of the emotional heart, whereas law is a tame and monochromatic pursuit of the rational brain. For reasons of social decorum, sex is commonly regarded as a private matter which is given a genteel social censorship – Gore Vidal said "I don't know if my first experience was heterosexual or homosexual because I was too polite to ask". So, when a sexual encounter is slowly inspected in a law court in minute detail, and in stilted language, the drama can become absurd.

Pearl Bailey once said "what the world really needs is more love and less paper work". As commendable an idea as that will seem in many quarters, it is true that human foibles will always generate a flow of legal cases and abundant paper work related to love and sex. In the chapter on this theme in the previous book in the series, *More Weird Cases*, the cases included one where a released prisoner in Italy tried to get back to prison to avoid living with his wife, a woman who sued a doctor for giving her involuntary orgasms, and a divorce granted on the basis that a man contemplated having an affair. Here are more curious cases of passion, advanced to the law for dispassionate resolution.

Oral contract

"Officer, would you look at these rubber genitals and tell the court whether they were the ones you were using on the night of 14th September, 2011". That is a line most lawyers wouldn't imagine they'd ever need to utter in court, but a lawyer for Christina Vavra in Manatee, Florida in 2011 may have had to ask just that question.

Police in Manatee County were carrying out a prostitution sting operation on the night of 14 September 2001, when 31-year-old Ms Vavra allegedly got into an undercover deputy's unmarked vehicle. Vavra's arrest report states that the undercover deputy asked how much it would cost for oral sex, to which she replied "You [go and] get however much you think you need". It seems she spoke that vaguely to avoid suggesting she was going to make an unlawful contract. The undercover deputy then drove to get cash and put several US$20 bills in a cupholder in the car. He asked her not take it all so he could have some money left for groceries. As they drove out of a car park, Ms Vavra reportedly asked the officer to expose his penis. The deputy opened his trousers and pulled out a flaccid rubber replica of a penis and then put a condom on it. Is this, you have to ask, something officers are trained to do at police college? Clearly, putting a condom on to a flaccid rubber penis fastened to your torso cannot be classed as an everyday skill. The crime report records that as Ms Vavra leaned over to perform oral sex on the officer an opossum ran out on to the road and the deputy had to slam on his brakes. Ms Vavra slid from her seat and cracked her head on the dashboard. The deputy then said he was uncomfortable having oral sex while driving. It seems that Ms Vavra, nursing her cracked head, was of the same opinion. So the officer then drove into another car park and again asked for a price. This time Ms Vavra allegedly replied "$20 for [oral sex]" at which point she was arrested.

Police use of the fake penis was legal but these items can be legally problematic in some situations especially if they are not flaccid. In 2004, Joanne Webb, a 43-year-old married woman, was arrested and charged by two undercover officers in Cleburne, Texas for possession of a number of rubber penises.

Mrs Webb was accused of organising private parties to sell items including rubber penises to female friends. She was indicted for selling items "designed or marketed as useful primarily for the stimulation of the human genital organs". The maximum sentence for this crime is a year in jail and a US$4,000 fine. In this case, however, the prosecution was eventually discontinued before trial.

Laws against consensual sexual activity arise from different philosophies. In the West, sex outside marriage was often seen as morally defective. Under the old regime in China, however, another view was once summed up in an edition of the *Peking Workers Daily*. It said sexual activity was wrong because it "consumes energy and wastes time", whereas "love of the Party and of the chairman, Mao-Tse-tung, takes no time at all and is in itself a powerful tonic".

Sometimes, consensual sexual activity has been difficult to prosecute unless another offence is also involved. In what must be one of the most bizarre regrets in legal history, J Edgar Hoover once lamented that "the FBI are powerless to act in cases of oral-genital intimacy, unless it has in some way obstructed interstate commerce".

Dangerous liaison

In Australia, a court ruled that a public servant from Canberra, who was injured while having sex with a friend in a motel room during a work trip, was entitled to workplace compensation.

In the Federal Court in 2012, Justice John Nicholas ruled that the claimant's injuries were sustained "in the course of her employment". During her sexual encounter, a lamp came away from the wall above the bed and she suffered injuries to her nose and mouth. The woman, suing as PVWY as her identity is protected, was employed in the human relations section of a Commonwealth government agency. The agency had sent her to a town in New South Wales where she was going to conduct budget reviews and train local staff. She was booked into a motel overnight. About a month earlier, the woman had met a man who lived in the town. They spoke several times on the phone and she made arrangements to meet up with him at the motel. How the light fitting became detached isn't specified in the case. In his statement, her friend said they were intensely engaged in their affections and could not be sure what happened. "I do not know", he said, "if we bumped the light or it just fell off". The woman applied for compensation for facial and psychological injury from ComCare, the federal government workplace safety body, but her claim was rejected. She then appealed, unsuccessfully, to the Administrative Appeals Tribunal. In the Federal Court, the woman's barrister, Leo Grey, said his client was at the motel at the behest of her employer and sex was "an ordinary incident of life" commonly undertaken in a motel room at night "just like sleeping or showering". Mr Grey referred to precedents including one where compensation was granted to a worker who slipped in the shower at a hotel. Andrew Berger, for ComCare, however, argued sex was not "an ordinary incident of an overnight stay like showering, sleeping or eating". Justice Nicholas ruled it was not necessary for the woman to show that the activity that led to the injury was one that had been expressly or impliedly induced or encouraged by her employer. His ruling stated that "If the applicant had been injured while playing a game of cards in her motel room she would be entitled to compensation even though it could not be said that her employer induced or encouraged her to engage in such an activity". Sexual activity was equivalent to any other lawful recreational activity.

The question of how careful at sex a person is legally required to be was examined in 2005 by the Massachusetts Appeals Court.

Early one morning, a man and woman were engaged in consensual sexual intercourse. During the passionate event, and "without the explicit prior consent" of the man, the woman suddenly manoeuvred herself in a way that caused her partner to suffer a penile fracture. The court ruled that while "reckless" sexual conduct might be actionable, merely negligent conduct would not be, and dismissed the man's case. Despite their general wisdom, neither juries nor judges, the court ruled, could be expected to decide if sexual activity had been executed with reasonable care.

Saddled with hard fortune

In the cult book, *Zen and the Art of Motorcycle Maintenance*, Robert Pirsig noted that a motorcycle is nothing but "a system of concepts worked out in steel".

According to the 2012 legal claim of Henry Wolf in California, his motorcycle featured some bad concepts. These defects were in the saddle design which, he argued, caused him to suffer an erection for over 20 months. He sought compensation in a San Francisco court from BMW North America, the bike manufacturer, and from Corbin-Pacific Inc. which manufactured the saddle fitted after the bike was originally produced. The plaintiff claimed that his injury began after a four-hour round trip in 2010 on his BMW motorcycle, with "a ridge like seat". His claim stated that his "severe case of priapism (a persistent lasting erection)" was caused by the seat on his motorcycle which was "negligently designed, manufactured and/or installed by defendants". For his 20-month ordeal, Mr Wolf claimed damages "in excess of $25,000 for negligence, loss of earnings, medical expenses, and emotional distress". The legal statement of claim filed with the court said he is "now is unable to engage in sexual activity, which is causing him substantial emotional and mental anguish".

Proving the causation between the "ridge like seat" and the plaintiff's condition might have been difficult. An American radio station interviewed a leading expert, Dr Michael Lutz, from the Michigan Institute of Urology, about the matters raised by the case. Dr Lutz said there were no medical data to support the plaintiff's claim. The doctor said that that compression of the neurovascular supply to the penis for a period of time "whether it be on a bicycle seat or some other device" can cause prolonged numbness of the genitalia but has not been implicated in cases of priapism.

Mr Wolf's problem is not one that appears widely in the law reports of most jurisdictions. A legal planning dispute in 2006 in the UK, however, touched on the same anatomical issue.

In Lancashire, Ray Kennedy's right to have his objection to a planning proposal registered was improperly denied several times. The matter had to be reheard after Rochdale Council eventually conceded that it was at fault. The council's computer system had persistently rejected Mr Kennedy's email submissions because they contained the word "erection". The word, a perfectly ordinary item of vocabulary in planning documents, was electronically deemed obscene, so the planning application was initially passed without any consideration of Mr Kennedy's objection.

Sex and the French city

The French attitude to making love is a matter of renown, but now there is judicial precedent from 2011 showing that a failure to deliver a reasonable sexual performance in a marriage can result in a claim for damages.

A civil appeals court in Aix-en-Provence awarded €10,000 damages to a wife for having to endure her ex-husband's sustained lack of sexual interest in her for several years. The award of compensation for "injurious abstinence" in *Monique v Jean-Louis B* was made under article 1382 of the French Civil Code. French law says that married couples undertake to lead a "shared communal life" and the appeals court ruled that this includes reasonable sexual consortium. Monique, 47, had brought the action following 21 years of marriage which she claimed were sexually unfulfilling. Her husband, 51, defended the allegation by arguing that there was significant sexual liaison albeit intermittent because of his health problems which included chronic fatigue arising from a heavy work schedule. The court rejected the husband's case. It stated that a sexual relationship between a husband and wife manifests the affection they have for one another and ruled "in this case it was absent". It found that the husband had failed to prove to the court that health problems were the reasons for his continuing abstinence from sex.

Historically, the English church courts would sometimes order a medical examination of a husband to determine whether he had the physical capacity to consummate a marriage. In 1778, for example, in a Canterbury case, penis inspectors were appointed by the court to evaluate the man's virility. The medical examination showed that the husband's manhood (known legally as his "virile member") was judged to be "soft and short". The court, however, noted that such flaccidity "does not always continue" (a man, after all, might not be fully aroused when being inspected by officers of the law) and ordered the marriage to run for three months before judgment could be conclusive.

In England, the matrimonial obligation is to maintain a "mutually tolerable sexual relationship" although even that doesn't apply across the life of a marriage. The old legalistic maxim that normal frequency of marital sex is "twice a week", expressed in the delicate maxim *bis ruere in hebdomade* (to disturb twice in seven) isn't concrete law.

As the seasoned family law judge, Lord Merriman, said in a case in 1947 "No one can sit here as long as I have sat without realising that there is the greatest diversity of standards between one set of spouses and another as to what is or is not a normal standard of sexual intercourse". In the 1947 case he ruled that a husband who had been prodigious in his sexual demands "sometimes even as much as five times in one night" and who had also made "certain revolting suggestions" to his wife about alternative sexual practices, was acting unreasonably. The major text on sex law says it would be unreasonable if "a husband insists on sex after every meal".

In 1960, the Court of Appeal ruled that a wife from Croydon was in breach of her marital obligations when, with great intolerance towards her husband who wasn't as sexually charged as she was, she repeatedly badgered him for sex. To rouse him into copulation she would, in the early hours of the morning "pull his hair, catch hold of him by the ears, and shake his head violently to and fro". By always eventually conceding to her demands, however, the husband was judged to have accepted her behaviour. So, no divorce for him – a crash helmet in bed was his only legal option.

Sunshine of his life

"I was sunbathing" is not a common defence in criminal courts. The 2011 case of Brian Bone at Stirling Sheriff Court was, therefore, an interesting development. Mr Bone, 50, was apprehended in a public place lying on a rug without any clothes except for frilly "buttock-revealing" knickers when he first advanced his sunbathing defence to officers. Giving evidence in the subsequent indecent exposure case in Scotland, PC Greg McKenzie said the event occurred when he and a colleague were in the city of Stirling patrolling at a site near a reservoir known to be used by couples and single men for sex. The court was told that the area near the reservoir was also popular with families taking part in outdoor activities such as horse riding, cycling and mountain biking. Constable Greg said "We turned a corner and this is where we observed Mr Bone. He was sat on a small clearing laid out on a rug". He told the court "We first thought he was completely naked but I noticed he was wearing what appeared to be women's underpants and they had his buttocks exposed". Community officer Steven Scott testified that "His underpants appeared to be a female's as they were frilly. The way he was posed, I thought he was there for sexual activity". Bone was also alleged to have his genitals exposed. He denied that and explained he was merely "topping up" his tan. Bone brought a pair of black pants to court and they were formally admitted as evidence in the trial. After taking testimony from the prosecution and defence, however, the court concluded they were the wrong pants. They were not, the court ruled, the pair Bone wore on the day in question. Sheriff Wyllie Robertson ruled that the sunbathing defence was incredible, found Bone guilty of the charge, and fined him £500.

Over time, law courts have been presented with various arguments that challenge belief. Previous cases have included one in which William G Halby, an American lawyer, argued that the US$111,364 he spent on prostitutes was for "therapeutic sex" to relieve osteoarthritis and sexual dysfunction, and that sum should be deducted from his tax bill as medical expenses.

The golden cup for unlikely defence must go, however, to Sunday Moyo, a 28-year-old man from Zimbabwe. When he was arrested for allegedly having sex with a donkey tied to a tree, Mr Moyo explained that the donkey was actually a prostitute who had changed herself into asinine form while they were having sex. When caught with the donkey in Zvishavane, about 200 miles south of the capital, Harare, Mr Moyo said he'd paid US$20 to a prostitute in a bar and was surprised by the turn of events their sexual encounter took. He was charged with bestiality. The preliminary hearing, however, hosted one of the most unusual lines to be delivered in a law court. Mr Moyo told the judge "I do not know what happened when I left the bar, but I am seriously in love with the donkey".

Examination fail

There is abounding advice about choosing a doctor. The writer Erma Bombeck once noted that one should "never go to a doctor whose office plants have died".

A case from 2011 shows that a woman should never go to a doctor who tells a patient that an internal examination will be "the most pleasurable experience of your life". Dr Priyantha Perera Kandanearachchi, who worked for

Cardiff and Abertawe Bro Morgannwg Health Boards, faced a disciplinary tribunal at the General Medical Council (GMC). Dr Kandanearachchi had performed an intimate internal procedure known as a "stretch and sweep" to help induce labour. Simon Jackson QC, counsel for the GMC, told the disciplinary hearing that the medical procedure required the patient to remove her lower clothing. Mr Jackson said the patient felt vulnerable and wasn't impressed when the doctor told her that the experience would be one of unparalleled pleasure. Mr Jackson said that at the end of the procedure the doctor had "patted her on the bottom". The doctor admitted the bottom patting but said it was to "reassure" her. Impropriety towards a midwife occurred when the doctor put both his arms around her waist. "He maintained his grip" Mr Jackson told the tribunal "and put his face against her left breast, pressing his mouth over the area of the nipple and made a kissing sound". Certainly, not a regular mode of professional interaction with a colleague. Stephen Climie, counsel for Dr Kandanearachchi, said the doctor's misconduct amounted to "17 seconds" and had to be weighed against 17 years in medicine. The GMC tribunal suspended the doctor for one year.

No prosecution concerning those incidents was brought but other more serious cases have involved some odd explanations. In a case from 1922, Vera Howley, a young woman from Liverpool, was given lessons in singing and voice production by Mr Owen Williams. In fact, Mr Williams, a Presbyterian choirmaster, had been engaging in sexual intercourse with her after telling her that it was a method of improving her voice. He was sentenced to seven years imprisonment.

Many allegations against doctors, however, turn out to be false.

In 2009, Bibi Giles sued her gynaecologist for having allegedly caused her to have raptures during a medical examination. The case, at Worcester County Court in England, was the first one in legal history to cite an intense "leg buckling orgasm" as a form of injury. Mrs Giles claimed she'd had two orgasms in less than two minutes and claimed damages of up to £50,000. She alleged that the doctor started stroking her in an intimate way and that she had an involuntary and sustained ecstatic reaction. The doctor, who had an impeccable clinical record, explained that he had done nothing wrong. In fact, Mrs Giles had sought sex from him but he had declined and reported her conduct to his medical colleagues. The case collapsed when a respected family doctor wrote to the court during the trial to say that when Mrs Giles had been his patient she had persistently harassed him for sex. Mrs Giles withdrew her claim against the gynaecologist and agreed to pay him £30,000 to cover his legal costs. Some singularly odd evidence was heard in this case. After successful pelvic surgery, a text message was sent from Mrs Giles to the doctor, whose first name is Angus, saying that "the new arrival needs christening with the Angus beef sausage". Mrs Giles claimed a friend had used her phone to send that text to encourage the doctor to consult her about a "fibroid problem". The court wasn't told by Mrs Giles, however, how a fibroid problem could be clinically treated with a beef sausage.

Not forever, ever

Personal relationships don't all mature well but some end more quickly than others, as a case in the United Arab Emirates demonstrated.

In Ras Al Khaimah Marriage Court in 2012, where the legal process works quicker than in most jurisdictions, a 20-year-old woman divorced her 80-year-old husband within an hour of being married. The marriage solemnisation was supposed to have taken place a week earlier but when the couple arrived they were told they would need to return with the young Pakistani bride's guardian to witness the ceremony. A week later, they came back with a witness and the marriage was consecrated. Less than 60 minutes later, however, the woman returned and requested that the same judge who had ordained the marriage should grant her a divorce from her octogenarian Emirati husband. The marriage must have suffered a particularly problematic initial 45 minutes but the nature of the problem is unknown. The woman did not give reasons in open court as to why she wanted a divorce. "The woman only insisted on being granted a divorce, saying she couldn't stay with the old man. She did not tell us why", a court official announced. Ending what seems to be the shortest marriage on historical record, the judge sought and gained the husband's consent and then ended the legal relationship. The woman returned the dowry to her former husband.

In England, Jerzy and Kathryn Sluckin were married at Kensington register office in November 1975. Within an hour, however, at the wedding reception, Kathryn surprised her friends and relatives by announcing "It won't work" and leaving. Kathryn was later found to be living in a Divine Light Meditation Commune in Finchley. Although factually ended after less than an hour, this wedding was not technically ended until over a year later, so the Emirati divorce is the quickest on record.

A case with similar facts to that of the one in Ras Al Khaimah was that of Anna Nicole Smith and her husband J Howard Marshall. Ms Smith met her husband while she was working as a topless model. She was 23 and he was 85. He was worth US$1.6 billion. They married in 1994 but she was never named in any will left by her husband, who died a year later. The marriage was described as "physically fulfilling". To get a slice of her late husband's estate, Ms Smith became involved in a court wrangle against her stepsons who, curiously, were old enough to be her grandparents. An award for unconventional perception must be given to Tom Cunningham, the lawyer who represented Ms Smith, for his opening courtroom line in the case about her husband's estate. "This is not about a gold-digger sucking money", Mr Cunningham boldly told the judges "this is about a relationship that was very profound".

A marriage of inconvenience

"Bigamy" observed the actor Bob Hope "is the only crime where two rites make a wrong". The crime of bigamy has been uncovered in many ways but a case from Washington State broke new ground.

In 2011, Alan O'Neill, a prison officer from Pierce County, was prosecuted after Facebook recommended that his two wives became friends. Mr O'Neill was married to Ellenora Fulk in 2001 but moved away in 2009. The couple were not divorced. When Ms Fulk was on Facebook, the "People You May Know" feature suggested a link to Teri Wyatt-O'Neill. When she clicked, she saw that her prospective new friend was posing in a profile picture next to Alan O'Neill and a wedding cake. Ms Fulk's suspicions were aroused. She called O'Neill's mother and about an hour later Alan O'Neill arrived back at his first wife's apartment, allegedly admitted that he had married again and begged her not to report him, saying that he'd fix everything. Ms Fulk, however, did not accede to that request. She reported him to the police and he was charged with bigamy. Pierce County Prosecutor Mark Lindquist noted that "Facebook is now a place where people discover things about each other they end up reporting to law enforcement". The crime carries a punishment of up to one year's imprisonment, a potentially awkward challenge for a prison officer. Mr O'Neill pleaded "not guilty" to the felony charge and was released on bail as the court accepted "the only danger he poses is marrying a third woman".

The courts have heard some odd reactions to bigamy allegations. One of the oddest was heard in the Family Court in Melbourne in 2008 – it is the story of four weddings and an annulment.

Mr Tristan – a pseudonym used in the law report – was married in 1966, but the marriage failed. Later, he met a Hawaiian woman, and fell in love. They got married and decided to live in Hawaii. They were prevented from resettling by the US Department of Homeland Security, which revealed that the marriage to the Hawaiian woman was invalid because Mr Tristan was already married. When Mr Tristan pointed out that he was divorced from his 1966 wife, the authorities said "no not her, the second woman you married, the one in Arizona in 1978". It was at this point that a shocked Mr Tristan said he dimly recalled a "nice blonde woman" and a 28-day party in Arizona while he was on shore leave as an oil rig cook in 1978.

He said, however, that he couldn't remember any details of the event. Memory is, indeed, likely to be impaired in anyone attending a 28-day party. Like Ross Geller in *Friends*, Homer Simpson, Britney Spears, and Dr Stu in *The Hangover*, Mr Tristan was intoxicated by more than love when he got hitched in a walk-in marriage service. Shown the 1978 Arizona marriage licence by which he had been wed to Ms Ernt (a legal pseudonym), he said "the sky fell in". He tried to track down his Arizona girl but could discover only that she had got married again in 1993, bigamously if she had not previously divorced him. At the Family Court, Justice Brown granted Mr Tristan an annulment of his 1978 marriage, saying that "he has no recollection of going through any ceremony of marriage ... or of discussing marriage, or of anything referable to marriage". In *The Devil's Dictionary*, Ambrose Bierce provides the following definition, "BIGAMY, n. A mistake in taste for which the wisdom of the future will adjudge a punishment called trigamy". Less cynically, the Australian legal system imposed no punishment on Mr Tristan.

Curbed enthusiasm

Items of furniture feature in many legal cases. So the centrality of a sofa to a 2012 case from the City of Waukesha, Wisconsin is unremarkable in itself. This case, however, involved the rare charge of "lewd and lascivious behaviour" with a yellow sofa on a public sidewalk.

Gerard P Streator, 46, was summoned to appear in court after an off-duty police officer jogging through the city at 11pm one evening found the man having sex with an abandoned couch situated on a curb. Mr Streator faced up to nine months' in prison and a US$10,000 fine. The police report stated that Ryan Edwards, an off-duty Waukesha police officer, was out for a jog when he spotted an abandoned couch on the curb. He observed a man, whom he later identified as Mr Streator, on the couch, thrusting his hips as if he was having sex with a person. The officer approached Streator to see what was going on and yelled "what are you doing?" which caused Mr Streator to jump up. The officer then noted two things in particular: that Mr Streator was facing him with an erect penis and that there was no one else on the couch. The officer chased Streator to an apartment complex. Although the officer was unable to gain access to the complex, he identified the apartment Mr Streator entered. When he returned with other officers the next day, Mr Streator's wife opened the door and said he was at work and that he had not been out the previous evening. Mr Streator later denied the charge.

There are some unusual precedents of people getting over-romantic with inanimate objects.

In 1989, a schoolmaster from London was convicted of "outraging public decency" after he was caught at the front of his classroom "going through the motions of sexual intercourse" on top of a desk.

In 1993, Karl Watkins was prosecuted for having sexual relations with pavements in Redditch.

In 2007, Robert Stewart was placed on probation for three years after being caught trying to have sex with a bicycle. The 51-year-old was naked from the waist down when two cleaners walked in on him at a hostel in Ayr.

In 2008, a 32-year-old man was arrested in Wiltshire for engaging in sexual activity with a lamp-post.

This sort of case has produced some unusual excuses. The most extraordinary of these was advanced by a construction worker from Poland who was caught on a London building site in an apparently sexual act with the tube of a Henry vacuum cleaner. When challenged by the shocked supervisor who caught him, he said that what he was doing was common practice in Poland, and that he was just cleaning his underpants.

Pole tax

In 2012, the Court of Appeals in New York decided that the spectacle of "women gyrating on a pole to music" cannot be classified as a "dramatic or musical arts performance" – a classification which is exempt from tax.

The court ruled that a club in Latham called Nite Moves would have to pay tax on its revenue, however "artistic or athletic" the moves of its dancers. The owners of the exotic dance club were appealing against a decision of the state's Tax Appeal Tribunal which had said the club was liable to pay US$124,000 in sales tax from revenue to the club between 2002 and 2005, plus interest. The owners argued that "exotic dance" should qualify for tax exemption because it is difficult to perform and requires practice and choreography. The Court of Appeals ruled, however, that the club failed to prove that performances on either its main stage or in private rooms qualified for the tax break. The court held against the club in a 4:3 majority ruling. It said that classifying the dances as artistic performances would allow all sorts of dubious acts to get tax exemption and that would defeat the purpose of the tax law. Ice shows "with intricately choreographed dance moves precisely arranged to musical compositions" had previously been denied a tax exemption, so pole dancing could definitely be declined dramatic and artistic status. In a dissent in favour of granting the tax exemption, Judge Robert Smith said that deciding the artistic merits of different dance forms "is not the function of a tax collector". He stated the people who paid admission charges paid to see women dancing, and "It does not matter if the dance was artistic or crude, boring or erotic". He concluded that "Under New York's tax law, a dance is a dance". He said the tribunal's ruling was wrong because it made "a distinction between highbrow dance and lowbrow dance" – a difference not noted in the relevant statute. Justice Smith made his point in a rather florid way. He said that personally, he would rather read the *New Yorker* than *Hustler* magazine but that he would be appalled "if the state were to exact from *Hustler* a tax that the *New Yorker* did not have to pay, on the ground that what appears in *Hustler* is insufficiently 'cultural and artistic'".

Arguments about the taxation of sexually related business have even extended to prostitution. In 1964, the Exchequer Court of Canada had to decide whether the expenses of running a "call girl" business in Vancouver were deductible from income tax. The woman who ran the business, along with seven call girls, were all convicted, imprisoned and taxed. They accused the authorities of hypocrisy for wanting a slice of immoral earnings.

But that was rejected by the court which then set about ruling what were permissible as tax-deductible expenses for this sex business. Expense claims concerning the ordinary parts of the business operation, like paying the telephone switchboard staff, were allowed. Some claims were rejected, however, but only because there was no proof that the money had been spent. The list included US$2,000 paid for liquor given to local government officials, and US$1,000 paid to "certain men possessed of physical strength and some guile, which they exercised when set to extricate a girl from difficulties".

Lastly, the court held that legal fees paid by the escort agency to lawyers defending the girls *were* necessary expenses and so tax deductible. This was an analysis as clinically commercial as the principle Mona Stangley, the famed brothel madam would declare to her firm's clients "it is always a business, doing pleasure with you".

A pretty difficult case

You can be fired for being consistently incompetent but can you be fired for being consistently attractive? Yes, according to the Iowa State Supreme Court in 2013, if the attraction threatens a marriage.

The court ruled that a dentist, Dr James Knight, acted lawfully when he dismissed Melissa Nelson, his dental assistant, because she was "irresistible". Mrs Nelson, a 32-year-old married mother of two, was dismayed by the ruling. She had worked for Dr Knight for ten years. Having occasionally made comments about Mrs Nelson's clothing being "too tight" and distracting, Dr Knight informed Mrs Nelson and her husband that he was dismissing her to protect his marriage because he feared that he might have an affair if she continued to work with him. During the final 18 months when Mrs Nelson was employed, Dr Knight at times asked her to put on her lab coat. In testimony he observed "I don't think it's good for me to see her wearing things that accentuate her body". Nelson denied that her clothing was tight or in any way inappropriate. Dr Knight acknowledged he once told Nelson that if she saw his trousers bulging, she would know her clothing was too revealing. Dr Knight's wife, Jeanne Knight, who also worked at the dental practice, insisted that her husband dismiss Nelson. Mrs Knight said "she was a big threat to our marriage". According to her affidavit and her deposition testimony, Mrs Knight had several complaints about Mrs Nelson. These included Mrs Nelson's texting with Dr Knight, her clothing and alleged flirting. Mrs Nelson's legal argument was not one of harassment but of gender discrimination. She said that Dr Knight fired her because of her gender and that he would not have fired her if she was male. The Supreme Court of Iowa rejected that argument and found in favour of Dr Knight on the basis that his decision was made on a personal basis, not on the basis of a sweeping gender discrimination. He was not against women as such – the replacement he hired after ending the contract of Mrs Nelson was also female. The court held that Dr Knight's decision was lawful because it was "driven entirely by individual feelings and emotions regarding a specific person" and was not a "gender-based" discrimination.

The law has previously had to deal with some odd allegations that a female body has triggered improper distraction. In 2011, in Chicago, attorney Thomas Gooch claimed that the buxom assistant to the lawyer on the other side of his case was distracting the jury. Mr Gooch was acting for a commercial client in a civil trial about a car purchase. Sitting at counsels' table with the opposing lawyer, Dmitry Feofanov, was a woman with a distinctly curvaceous figure. The woman, Daniella Atencia, was dressed, Gooch argued, "in such a fashion as to call attention to herself". He requested Judge Anita Rivkin-Carothers to order the woman to sit in the gallery with members of the public so that she would not distract jurors with the size of her chest. In remarks that suggested the only anatomical concern she had with Mr Gooch related to the size of his brain, the judge offered a criticism of his approach and the lawyer withdrew his request.

Freedom of sexpression

In 1791, the First Amendment to the US Constitution, setting out the right of freedom of speech, was adopted in the Bill of Rights.

The notion of freedom of speech has since been extended several times to include "expressive conduct" as opposed to just the use of words. In 1969, the Supreme Court held that it was unconstitutional for a high school to suspend students for wearing black armbands to protest against the Vietnam War because their conduct was "akin to pure speech" and didn't interfere with the rights of other students.

A case in California in 2013 sought to extend the First Amendment to cover an altogether different type of conduct: having sex on film without the use of condoms. A group of plaintiffs from the pornography industry sued to challenge a law that required condom use on film sets. They argued that unprotected sex is a form of free expression. As part of voting in the US general election, electors in Los Angeles County endorsed a new law known as "Measure B" or the Safer Sex in the Adult Film Industry Act. Under the law, producers of pornography have to apply and pay for a permit from the Los Angeles County Department of Health before filming pornography. They are also subject to random inspections to check if the male performers are wearing condoms. Those who don't comply can be fined. "The idea of allowing a government employee to come and examine our genitalia while we're on set is atrocious", Amber Lynn, an adult film actress, told a local news channel. The regulations previously applied only in the city of Los Angeles but now apply throughout Los Angeles County. The new law was supported by the AIDS Healthcare Foundation, which argued that condoms would help protect the performers. The litigation was brought by Vivid Entertainment, Califa Productions and 'Jane and John Doe', legal aliases to confer anonymity on porn actors whose stage names were Kayden Kross and Logan Pierce. They sued Los Angeles County, its district attorney and its director of public health, claiming the new law violates the First

Amendment because the transfer of sexually transmitted diseases is a "constitutionally protected expression". The plaintiffs argued that the new law threatens the livelihood of 10,000 Angelenos, pornography makers and porn actors because the market for their films would disappear rapidly if they depict sexual activity involving condoms.

Although the law in many countries regards the use of condoms as important as a matter of public policy, there are limits to how far the law will take this strategy.

In Darwin, Australia in 2004, Lee Collinson was prosecuted for driving without a licence. When pulled over by police, Mr Collinson, 24, protested that he was on a critical mission of necessity to deliver a bag containing condoms to his cousin. Using a direct style of Australian English, he testified "My cousin was about to [have sex with] this girl and he needed his bag because it had his condoms in it". He argued that he committed the offence of driving without a licence from necessity. The magistrate acknowledged the urgency of Collinson's undertaking for his friend in need, commending it as good "mateship". The Bench then tried to demonstrate its magisterial understanding of the human situation by quoting a Spike Milligan remark about the strength of passion "at boiling point". But the heat of passion does not melt driving law so Collinson was convicted and fined AUS$100.

Bonded in bed

In her *Desultory Thoughts and Reflections* in 1839, the Countess of Blessington said that marriages are formed "by people who pay for a month of honey with a life of vinegar". In India, a High Court judge gave a ruling that for some people will give that idea the force of law.

In the High Court in Madras in 2013, in *Aysha v Ozir Hassan*, Justice CS Karnan ruled that a sexual relationship between consenting adults of marriageable age is sufficient to constitute a marriage. If applied throughout the state of Tamil Nadu, with 72 million people, the ruling would, overnight, so to speak, create many more marriages than had been planned. The case concerned the issue of monthly maintenance payments but involved a challenge to the validity of a marriage. Ruling that there was a valid marriage in this case, the court stated that "If the couple chooses to consummate their sexual cravings, then the act becomes a total commitment with adherence to all consequences that may follow ...". Justice Karnan stipulated that "the usual marriage formalities such as tying of thaali, exchange of garlands, exchanging rings and circling around [a] matrimonial fire pit or registering at a registration office" were mere rites "to comply with certain religious customs and for the satisfaction of society". It was sex, he ruled, that was the triggering point of legal marriage.

The odd ruling threw lawyers into some degree of apprehension. If the Karnan principle is applied in future, it will be impossible in many cases to have reliable evidence on something so important as whether a couple were married. Geetha Ramaseshan, a prominent advocate and women's rights activist, noted that "You cannot force someone to be in a relationship just because they were in a sexual relationship once. Many people change their partners often even before marriage". One rationale of the judgment was to deter men from engaging women in sexual relationships unless they intend to be bonded for life. Mr Justice Karnan later said his ruling would help maintain the "cultural integrity of India" and "protect the welfare of women". How far that will work is an open question. Another possible consequence of the ruling was touched on after the judgement by D Prasanna, president of the Women's Lawyers Association. She said some girls "may use promiscuous relationship[s] for exploiting a financially sound person".

There are other examples of unusually forged marriage. In 2009, the parents of a 14-year-old girl in Israel were surprised to learn one evening, when they asked her about school that day, that she had got married. The girl and her 17-year-old husband had married according to traditional Jewish law which requires three criteria to be satisfied. A wedding vow must be made in front of at least two witnesses, the husband must give his betrothed a ring, and the relationship must be consummated. The ardent couple satisfied the requirements in a venture that began in the school playground. The couple's union was later consummated – a liaison which is legal under Israeli secular law as sexual relations with a 14-year-old are not criminal if the male partner is no more than three years older than the female. The couple, however, were later divorced at the Rabbinical Court of Jerusalem.

In Scotland, historically until 1940, if a woman proved that she had allowed herself to be seduced on the promise of marriage, then the actual "act of seduction" could constitute a form of marriage. If, during that era, a man asked the woman after the seduction "How was it for you?", she could reply "it was truly nuptial, darling".

Chapter 3

Food, Drink and Drugs

Every year, the law courts of the world digest many cases related to food and drink, and are stimulated by many arguments about drugs. The mixture of food and regulations can be something of a recipe for oddity. "This rock salt is over 200 million years old", read the label on one container, "formed through ancient geological processes in the German mountain ranges. Best before 01-05-2013".

Alcohol, although a source of pleasure for many, has fuelled more law cases, in one way or another, than any other substance. Licensing cases, road traffic cases, street fights, domestic violence, and even drunken lawyers behaving chaotically in courts have all been generated by drink. The nature of the issue was neatly encapsulated once by Homer Simpson in a toast to liquor "To alcohol! The cause of, and solution to, all of life's problems". The wry writer PG Wodehouse said that "Alcohol is a misunderstood vitamin". In any event, it is an elixir not unknown in the professional world, a phenomenon captured in the line of Robert Benchley "Often Daddy sat up very late working on a case of Scotch".

Drugs continue to challenge the courts with some unusual cases, and to divide society into many viewpoints, including the unconventional. Mick Miller, the British entertainer has said, "I don't like people who take drugs – customs men, for example".

The chapter on this theme in the previous book in the series, *More Weird Cases*, included a case in which a customer's withering critique of an apple tart in a French shop lead to a two-year criminal case of "public insult", a girl who texted her friend to come round to smoke some dope but mis-keyed and randomly messaged an officer from the Drugs Task Force, a man prosecuted for 'assault with a dangerous sausage' during a food fight at a dinner party, and a Swiss case which required a Bench of judges to drink alcopops as part of their evaluation of the dispute. Here are more cases to sample.

Joint enterprise

In 2011, a 34-year-old man from Edinburgh faced jail after indignantly reporting to the police that someone had stolen his prized cannabis plants.

The writer William Burroughs once noted that "there isn't a feeling you can get on drugs that you can't get without drugs". But David Williamson strongly disagreed, and when police arrived at his home after a disturbance he reported that he had been robbed of two valuable cannabis plants that he had cultivated to just the strain he liked best. Prosecuting at Edinburgh Sheriff Court, Fiscal Depute Dev Kapadia said that once they had been told of the stolen plants, police officers thought that "there may be some production ongoing" and obtained a search warrant. The court heard that 20 plants worth £3,000, some seedlings worth about £900, and cultivating equipment were recovered from Williamson's home. Williamson admitted ownership of the cultivation and told police that he grew his own cannabis "to feed his habit". In court, Williamson's defence agent, Robbie Burnett, said his client, who suffers from hepatitis C, was an authority on cannabis. Mr Burnett said that during the police interview his client "demonstrated a remarkably detailed knowledge of cannabis – the different strains and the different purposes to which it could be put". Mr Williamson discovered that if he grew a particular strain he could suppress the hepatitis C syndrome.

There are over 250 illegal drugs in the UK ranging from simple cannabis to the less simple α-Methylphenethylhydroxylamine. Cannabis, however, accounts for more drug-related arrests (80 per cent) than those made for all other illegal substances put together. According to a Home Office British Crime Survey published in October, 2007, 2.6 million people between the ages of 16 and 59 used cannabis in the previous year.

Some countries adopt a particularly strict approach to policing the drug. In 2007, in Dubai, a British citizen, Keith Brown, was sentenced to four years' imprisonment for possession of 0.003 grams of cannabis, about the weight of a grain of sand.

A number of startling defences to drugs charges have challenged courts.

After being caught in possession of marijuana in France in 2010, Michel Rouyer, a duck farmer, pleaded the unprecedented defence of "ducking necessity". He said that marijuana was something he gave to his ducks medicinally to deworm them. His lawyer told the Bench "This is for real, not one [duck] has worms and they're all in excellent health". Rouyer was fined €500 and given a one-month suspended sentence.

In 2007, a defendant was shown leniency after explaining that the cannabis he had been caught growing was for him to use to soothe a chronic genital itch. Gregor Spalding, 30, admitted cultivating the drug at his home in Blairgowrie, Scotland. The sentence was deferred for six months for him "to be of good behaviour". He was told that if he kept within the law for six months he'd be treated leniently: a great challenge for someone who might well have been itching to break the law.

The most bizarre defence given by someone apprehended with drugs, however, was offered in Florida. Raymond Stanley Roberts was arrested for possession of two plastic bags which police found up his bottom. Roberts said that a plastic bag, containing cannabis, which was the first bag police pulled out of him, was his but that he knew nothing about the second bag they pulled out, which contained cocaine.

The mousse that was a trifle

An old legal principle says *de minimis non curat lex* – the law takes no account of trifling matters. Mousses, however, are a different matter.

An NHS Trust which tried to deduct £84,450 from the money it owed to a food supplier because of a single day-old chocolate mousse lost its case. In 2012, a High Court contract case heard how Mid Essex Hospital Services NHS Trust tried to withhold, in total, over £700,000 from the private catering firm, Medirest. Mr Justice Cranston ruled that the deductions, including one for £96,060 for a few three-day old bagels, were "patently absurd". He ruled that neither the trust nor the catering firm could win damages claims after their contract ended in acrimony. In April 2008, Medirest won a multimillion-pound contract to supply meals for seven years at St John's and Broomfield hospitals in Essex. The deal collapsed, however, after only 18 months when the trust made repeated complaints and, at one point, tried to deduct £716,197 from the caterer's routine financial entitlements. Mr Justice Cranston condemned the deductions as "ridiculously high", noting that they included £46,320 deducted for a box of out-of-date ketchup sachets found in a cupboard, and £84,450 for the single day-old chocolate mousse. Mr Justice Cranston ruled that Medirest was entitled to end the contract because the trust had breached the agreement and failed to "co-operate in good faith". It had also exercised its contractual power in "an arbitrary, capricious and irrational manner". He also accepted that the trust had the right to end the contract because Medirest had "accumulated the requisite number of service failure points". He ruled that neither the trust nor Medirest could win their claims for losses after the contract was ended.

Previously, the oddest legal case over a relatively small food matter occurred in France in 2010. What began as an unkind comment about the way sliced apples were arranged on the top of a tart in a bakery triggered a two-year legal battle which ended in the criminal courts.

The events began in April 2008 when a woman and her daughter went into a bakery in Nogent-sur-Marne in

Paris. The woman made a withering criticism of the way
the baker, Christelle, had patterned the many crescent-
shaped apple slices on the surface of a tarte aux pommes.
Her denunciation of the tart was so vehement, the
dismayed baker responded by saying *"quelle conne"* (what
a stupid bitch). The customer's indignation at this insult
was even worse than her indignation at the tessellated
tart. She invoked a piece of legislation from 1881 to
prosecute the baker for making a "public insult" – an
offence with a maximum fine of €12,000. Once the public
insult charge had been made, the judge was obliged to
ask a magistrate to conduct an investigation. The criminal
justice apparatus was then set in motion so the baker
was interrogated by police, witnesses were examined
and the case thoroughly prepared. Two years after the
argument in the shop, the public insult charge finally
came to trial. The baker, Christelle, appeared before the
11th correctional chamber of Chéteil ready to defend
herself. However, when prosecutors took their case out
of the oven it was seen to be half-baked and it collapsed.
The complainant shopper failed to attend court, so two
years of prosecution work were wasted. The case was
dismissed. What the prosecutor then called the shopper
can only be imagined.

Mucking fadness

Following a lawyer's contention about the use of the
word "fuck" in Australia, a savoury snack called "Nuckin
Futs" became registered as a trademark in 2012. In 2011,
the trademark application for "Nuckin Futs" was rejected
as being scandalous and offensive as it is similar to the
phrase "fucking nuts". The registrar ruled that "Nuckin
Futs" was an "obvious spoonerism" and held the name
was ineligible for registration under section 42 of the
Trade Marks Act. The law states that trade names must be
rejected if likely to be regarded as shameful, offensive or
shocking to the ordinary person. The case was appealed
by Jamie White, a solicitor and director of the law firm Pod
Legal, who argued for his corporate client on the Gold
Coast, Queensland, that "Nuckin Futs" wasn't offensive

because the words "fuck" or "fucking" are "now part of the universal discourse of the ordinary Australian". Mr White's argument stated "We submit that whilst there may be a mere sentimental objection or mere distaste to NUCKIN FUTS, this is not a sufficient ground for rejection of the Trade Mark, particularly since a substantial number of people would not find the words shocking". He noted, out of court, that, over time, "certain words which may have caused major offence in earlier times would now be acceptable as trade marks in certain markets, namely, the Australian market". On appeal, the Trademark Examiner agreed to register the "Nuckin Futs" trademark on the condition that the owner would not market the product to children. Mr White gave an assurance that his client's product, nuts with added flavouring, would be sold only in pubs, nightclubs and other adult venues.

Since its first recorded use in 1503, the word "fuck" and its grammatical variants has become progressively widely used. Its first appearance in law reports came in a case decided by the Supreme Court of the State of Missouri in 1846. Mr McCutchen sued Mr Edgar for slander. The "slanderous charge" the law report notes was "carnal knowledge of a mare", and "the word [fuck] was used to convey the imputation". The plaintiff insisted he hadn't had any carnal connection with a mare, and he won his action. The defendant appealed saying that the word "fuck" was "unknown to the English language" and "was not understood by those to whom it was spoken" so there could have been no slander. The appeal court, however, ruled in favour of the plaintiff. It said "the modesty of our lexicographers restrains them from publishing obscene words" or from giving "obscene signification" to some words but "it does not follow that they are not English words, and not understood by those who hear them".

The ground breaking "nuckin futs" case isn't the first time the legal boundaries of language have been declared to be liberal in Australia. In 1999, the Supreme Court of Victoria held that in modern Australia one can be quite robust in one's critique of a judge.

A solicitor who had been served with an injunction, said "Justice Beach has got his hand on his dick". The court held that "The matter must be judged by contemporary Australian standards. It may be offensive, but it is not contempt of court, for a person to describe a judge as a 'wanker'.

Lines of electoral persuasion

In the UK, cases of electoral misconduct run from the 1430s. For centuries, malpractice like bribery was common. Samuel Pepys, for example, paid £8 to 32 electors in Harwich in 1689.

The types of electoral misconduct known to the world were extended by a scheme that featured in a court case in Brazil in 2012. A politician was arrested for allegedly handing out cocaine with her election leaflets. Ms Carme Cristina Lima, 32, was running to be a city councillor in Itacoatiara, in the northern state of Amazonas. The suspicions of the police were aroused when they saw a crowd allegedly thronging around Ms Lima's car on the morning of the election day. It looked like she might have been delivering more than promises not to raise taxes. Police officers searched her car and allegedly found hundreds of packets of cocaine attached to the candidate's leaflets with instructions on how to vote for her. Police chief Daniel Ottoni said "There was a large gathering of people around Ms Lima, but when they saw the police they all ran away". The candidate and another man also fled by car but officers caught up with them. Chief Ottoni said that according to locals, Ms Lima had been distributing the drugs since early in the morning "on condition that people vote for her". Lima was charged with electoral corruption and drug dealing.

The use of cocaine as an unorthodox system of payment has occurred in other fields and has even affected lawyers.

Nicholas Athanasiou, an attorney in Colorado, was implicated in one of the largest drug gangs to be caught in the history of the state. In police raids, 97 homes were searched and the material seized included an SKS assault rifle, an AR-15 assault rifle and handguns; US$415,140 in cash; 26,129 grams of cocaine; 1,000 grams of crack cocaine; and one pound of methamphetamine. Following

Mr Athanasiou's admission at a professional disciplinary hearing to possession of a controlled substance, he was suspended from the practice of law for a period of one year and one day. While clinically noting that Mr Athanasiou's misconduct constituted grounds for the imposition of "discipline pursuant to C.R.C.P. 251.5 and violated Colo. RPC 1.7(a)(2), 1.8(a), and 8.4(d) and (h)", the report of the hearing ends with the more concerning fact that the charges stemmed "from his acceptance of cocaine on several occasions from his client as payment for his legal fees".

52 bottles of whiskey

The doctor and poet, Oliver St John Gogarty, is credited with the epigram that "there is no such thing as a small whiskey".

In an unusual case in Scottdale, Pennsylvania in 2013, prosecutors alleged that John Saunders succumbed to the temptations of whiskey in a big way – by drinking 52 bottles of it that belonged to his employer. The bottles were a century old and valued at US$102,400. Mr Saunders was a live-in caretaker at a large Georgian mansion when it was bought by Patricia Hill in 2012. She purchased the building, which had been owned by the coal magnate JP Brennan, to renovate it and convert it into a bed and breakfast hotel. During the renovations, nine cases, containing a total of 102 bottles of Old Farm Pure Rye Whiskey, were discovered secreted in the wall and the stairwell. The whiskey had been distilled in 1912 and bottled in 1917. By 1917, over half the states in the United States had prohibited alcohol and the national prohibition was on the horizon. Ms Hill speculated, after finding the hidden stash of alcohol, that Mr Brennan, who had been known to like a drink, had been taking precautions against the impending alcohol ban when he hid the boxes. Ms Hill told the police that Mr Saunders had helped her brush the dust off the cases, which contained 12 bottles each, and store them in a living room. She said after Mr Saunders later moved out, she discovered that 52 bottles had become empty. Mr Saunders, 62, was charged with receiving stolen property and theft. He initially told the authorities that he had not drunk the whiskey, saying that it must have evaporated. Later, however, police matched his DNA to DNA found on the mouths of three empty bottles.

The law has dealt with large quantities of alcohol in some unusual cases. The memorably titled *The King v Forty Nine Casks of Brandy* (1836) concerned an event in which casks of brandy came ashore on the south coast of England near Poole in Dorset. The case involved a dispute between the estate of William Bankes, a local property owner, and the King as to who had the best title to the goods. The relevant area of law contains many fine distinctions. For example, to constitute "wreck of the sea", and thus be subject to one set of rules, the goods must have "touched the ground", though they need not have been left dry. Goods on the high seas, however, if they have not touched the ground are "droits" like flotsam and jetsam, and are subject to a different set of rules. In the brandy case, 49 casks had been taken to the Custom House at Weymouth. These were divided into categories according to where they had been seized, and assigned by the court, variously to the King and the estate of Bankes, according to the rules. It is not recorded how the litigants celebrated their gains.

Judges themselves have sometimes given opinions demonstrating that not all their time is spent reading law reports. In a tax case from Ireland in 1894, about whether drinks at a local council lunch were legitimate expenses, Chief Justice O'Brien referred with some evident personal knowledge to "two dozen bottles of champagne, Ayala 1885 – a very good brand, one dozen Marcobrunn Hock – a very nice hock, one dozen Château Margaux – an excellent claret, one dozen bottles of fine old Dublin whiskey – the best whiskey that can be got, six bottles of Amontillado sherry – a stimulating sherry; and ... some more fine Dublin whiskey!".

It is sometimes difficult to deny the observation of Charles Dickens in 1859 that the law is "certainly not behind any other learned profession in its Bacchanalian propensities".

A criminal recipe

It is unusual for personal misconduct with food to become a federal case. But the prosecution of Anthony Garcia in Albuquerque, New Mexico in 2011, was decidedly unusual.

Mr Garcia was indicted for having fed semen, disguised as yoghurt, to an unsuspecting shopper while giving out food samples in the supermarket where he was working. There are many hundreds of volumes of US federal law but nowhere is there a direct precedent for this case. Garcia, 32, was working at the Sunflower Market when he offered the "yogurt" to shoppers to taste. He approached one woman who agreed to sample some, and she took the spoon that he proffered. After tasting the sample, she immediately spat it out on the floor saying it was "gross and disgusting" and that it tasted like semen. The woman also wiped her mouth on the garment she was wearing to get the taste out of her mouth. Police were called and they collected samples of the woman's spit from the floor and took the garment she was wearing as evidence. The police obtained a search warrant and collected blood and DNA samples from Garcia. They then matched sperm cells found in both the victim's saliva and on the garment to Garcia using DNA. Investigators with the US Food and Drug Administration argued that Garcia falsely claimed not to know that the spoon he handed the customer contained semen. Garcia was arrested and indicted for adulterating food and making false statements to federal investigators. In a statement that even the best defence counsel would find hard to dispute, the prosecutor, Kenneth Gonzales, said "No one should have to endure this type of experience simply because she or he accepts a food sample while shopping for groceries". Garcia pleaded guilty on both charges and was sentenced to two years imprisonment.

Contaminating food with other bodily fluids has been known in English law. Section 38 of the Public Order Act 1986 makes it an offence to contaminate or interfere with goods with the intention of "causing public alarm or anxiety".

In 2009, Richard Benjamin Shannon was working at the sandwich chain Subway in Brownhills in the Midlands. For reasons he later found hard to explain, Shannon took pieces of lettuce from one of the serving trays, put some of them up his nose and then chewed on others before replacing them all in the tray. That was clearly a salad dressing of which customers would be unaware. His exploits were filmed by a friend on a mobile phone and then posted on YouTube. In a bizarre twist, Shannon was only arrested by police later after an incident in which an irate woman who recognised him from the YouTube film went to the Subway where he worked and hurled a chair at him. The film of Shannon's conduct with the lettuce was viewed by Walsall Magistrates' Court during his trial. The court could have sentenced Shannon to six months in prison, but acknowledged his remorse and guilty plea and ordered him to do 300 hours of unpaid work for the community.

In Henry VIII's reign, contaminating food was something for which the culprit could also be punished in the community. For poisoning the soup of the Bishop of Rochester in 1530, a man called Rose was taken to Smithfield in London where he was publicly boiled to death in front of the community.

Do you want sprinkles?

The website of Lickety Split Ice Creams says that the firm was founded in 2003 by Joe Patty II, a Memphis police officer, because he wanted to provide "ice cream from a truck that parents could trust".

Most of the time that has been true but it wasn't in the case of Louis Scala. The Lickety Split truck from which he sold ice cream across Staten Island was also the retail outlet for his US$1m drug-trafficking ring. In 2011, he was sentenced to three-and-a-half years in prison by Judge Jill Korviser on one count of conspiracy and one count of criminal possession of a controlled substance. The core business plan of Mr Scala revolved around selling oxycodone, a prescription painkiller that produces an addictive high similar to that of heroin. While driving around and offering such treats as the Strawberry Shortcake ice lolly and the Nutzo cornet to children from the serving hatch, Scala invited adults into the back of the truck to buy his special sprinkles. He obtained the drugs with a prescription pad stolen by his accomplice from the office of a Manhattan doctor. Using over 20 "runners", Scala obtained nearly 43,000 oxycodone pills between July 2009 and June 2010. The prosecution noted that each pill, known by the brand name OxyContin, had a street value of US$20.

Other unconventional retail sales in the US have also ended in court. In San Jose, California, Jose Gilberto Ortiz was arrested for offering unusual side dishes from his hotdog stand: machine guns and sawn-off shotguns. His assistant on the stand was also keen to help customers but he wasn't so much about mustard as methamphetamine. Both men were arraigned in the US District Court.

In another bizarre case, Elizabeth Hunt was indicted on drugs charges for putting two grams of marijuana in the Subway order of anyone if they used a special code by asking for "extra meat" and then putting a US$10 bill in the tips jar. In their affidavit, undercover investigators for the sheriff's office allege that Ms Hunt, a "sandwich artist" at Subway in Fort Pierce, Florida, slipped them a bag of marijuana on two occasions when they used the code. Hunt faced two charges of sale and delivery of marijuana within 1,000 feet of a convenience store, possession of marijuana with intent to sell within 1,000 feet of a convenience store and possession of drug paraphernalia.

Historically, however, drugs were sold as part of standard retailing. In the 1880s, Parke, Davis & Co, a major American manufacturer of cocaine, sold the drug in 15 forms including coca-leaf cigarettes and cheroots, cocaine inhalant, a Coca Cordial, cocaine crystals, and in a cocaine injection kit complete with a hypodermic needle. The company promised that its cocaine products would "supply the place of food, make the coward brave, the silent eloquent and render the sufferer insensitive to pain".

Before 1903, the Coca-Cola Company, which sold Coke as a "brain tonic", put cocaine into its drink. As

Justice Holmes said in a judgment in 1920, the popularity of the beverage was helped "by the presence of cocaine, a drug that, like alcohol or caffeine or opium, may be described as a deadly poison or as a valuable item of the pharmacopoea". Putting a small part of cocaine in the drink was, clearly, a reasonably effective way to keep customers coming back for more.

Cereal killers

If you are in jail pending a charge of aggravated murder, do you have a constitutional right to Cocoa Puffs? Lawyers in a case in Washington State in 2012 spent over two hours on their feet arguing that there is such a right.

Holly Grigsby and David "Joey" Pedersen were accused of killing Pedersen's father and stepmother, David "Red" Pedersen and DeeDee, in Everett. The suspects, who had connections with white supremacist groups, were also being investigated in relation to two other killings. Pedersen and Grigsby, who both appeared in shackles at a preliminary hearing, had been classified as maximum security inmates because of the nature of the charges against them and the fact they had taken flight from justice across three states before being caught. The maximum security classification means that the prisoners are denied access to the jail's store from which Cocoa Puffs are available. The state argues that allowing prisoners like Pedersen and Grigsby access to snacks is a security issue. Such snacks can be used as currency for favours and sugary products can be utilised for making the alcoholic drink known as jailhouse hooch. Since being jailed, Grigsby had violated regulations several times including incidents of trying to brew alcohol in her cell and of trying to communicate with Pedersen through a mail scam. Grigsby's defence attorney, Pete Mazzone, in a lengthy submission, contended that it was against his client's constitutional rights to deny her access to the jail store, and that a bowl of Cocoa Puffs could not amount to a security risk.

Prison food featured in another odd case in 2009. Under an Alabama law passed in 1927, sheriffs were allocated

US$1.75 to feed each prison inmate per day. The sheriffs, however, were allowed to spend less than that full amount on prisoners' food and to pocket the difference.

The sum of US$1.75 bought a reasonable amount in 1927 but it didn't buy much in 2009, so, when a County Sheriff, Greg Bartlett, tried to maximise his profit turn from the US$1.75, he took the idea of "economic meals" further than the law permits. Bartlett was jailed for starving the prisoners in his Morgan County jail. He testified that, supplementing his annual salary of US$64,000, he made an additional US$212,000 in personal income over three years by siphoning off "excess" from his prisoners' food budget. In 2001, in a federal legal action about conditions for Morgan County prisoners, a settlement was made which required inmates to be given the minimum of "nutritionally adequate meals". In 2009, however, a federal judge found evidence of continuing endemic malnourishment among prison inmates, and he jailed the sheriff for contempt of court. The judge heard how the sheriff had put about half of the public money allocated for prisoners' food into his own bank account while feeding 300 men and women prisoners things such as bloody chicken and cold grits. Ten emaciated prisoners testified before the federal judge saying things such as "we had an apple at Christmas". Sheriff Greg Bartlett was sent to his own jail. There is no mention of what welcoming party, if any, his inmates threw for him when he arrived among them as a fellow inmate. A party might have been difficult, of course, as the inmates would have been a bit short of food and drink.

The proof of the pudding is in court

Black pudding is a blend of onions, pork fat, oatmeal, and blood – usually from a pig. Some people love it and others do not. In 800 years of reported cases, black pudding has appeared in only two British legal cases. One in 1929 was about rates, and one in 1958 that decided a slaughterhouse can be classified as a factory.

Then, in a case from Perth in Scotland in 2012, the black pudding featured in another part of the law – the criminal law. Mr Bradley Davidson, 47, was accused of committing a crime with a black pudding at his flat in May, and appeared at Perth sheriff court in a preliminary hearing. The charge said "[You] behaved in a threatening or abusive manner which was likely to cause a reasonable person to suffer fear and alarm in that you did act in an aggressive manner, shout and throw a black pudding across the room". Mr Davidson also faced a charge of assaulting a girl on the same date by kicking her on the leg, and a third charge alleged that he damaged property by kicking a door. Mr Davidson denied the charges and the Crown eventually discontinued the case, clearing him on all counts.

In 2011, English law faced the issue of whether a sausage could be a significant missile. Prosecutor Richard Stevens told Chelmsford Crown Court that at a dinner party there had been "unruly horseplay involving a number of people before the sausage came into the scene". Ashly Brearey had been formally charged with assault causing actual bodily harm to Candice Whybrow. The particulars of the offence were that he was alleged, at his home in Tithelands, dangerously to have thrown a sausage at his victim during a food fight. Collectively, the judge and all the lawyers in the case had spent about 80 years studying and practising law so they were well-prepared for a trial of "assault with a dangerous sausage".

After some courtroom argument about whether the injurious missile was, in fact, a sausage or a chicken drumstick which had been found on the carpet, the judge suggested the case should be discontinued. The prosecution accepted his advice so the finer points of sausage assault law were not determined.

Earlier, however, in 2008, a Scottish court confirmed that, legally, a pineapple can be an "agent of harm". A former policewoman who was struck on the sternum by a flying pineapple during a disturbance was awarded £3,000 damages.

Pastry missiles have also been the subject of judicial attention. The Supreme Court of Canada heard a case in 2009 about an arrest for "possession of a pie with unlawful intent". Police said they believed that someone in Vancouver was going to throw a pie at the Canadian Prime Minister. They arrested Cameron Ward. Although Ward was clearly pieless when stopped, acting on a suspicion that he might be "hiding pies", officers whisked him to jail where he was stripped and given a thorough personal search. No pies. He was then locked in a tiny cell for four and a half hours. In court, a police officer who was asked whether she had found any evidence that Ward was guilty of pie-related offences mysteriously replied "I did not come across any evidence that he was not". Ward sued the police and won. He was found not to have violated any part of the law of pies.

Putting a foot wrong

In law, keeping consistent standards is very important. In a renowned remark in 1617, the jurist John Selden said that if law could be simply altered by any given Lord Chancellor according to his conscience, "one might as well make the standard measure of one foot the Chancellor's foot". No one disputes the exact 12-inch measure of a foot, and that is the basis of a claim which was filed in the Supreme Court in New Jersey in 2013.

Two men claimed that the "Footlong" Subway sandwiches they regularly purchased were, in fact, only 11 inches long. John Farley and Charles Noah Pendrack sued Subway for compensatory damages and for a change in its business practices. They argued that they had been sold short by 5 percent to 8.3 per cent on each Footlong sandwich they purchased, and they applied for triple damages for the deliberate and systematic nature of the alleged wrong. So, the claim amounted to US$1.23–US$1.62 per Footlong sandwich purchased. The plaintiff's lawyer, Stephen DeNittis, argued that Subway should make their "Footlongs" a foot long or stop advertising them as such. The implications of the case were huge because there are 38,000 Subway outlets worldwide and over a hundred million Footlongs are sold annually. Mr DeNittis said that "the case is about holding companies to deliver what they've promised". Gathering evidence, he purchased Footlongs from 17 shops, photographing each one beside a ruler, and every one was shorter than 12 inches.

There is a legal principle known as *de minimis non curat lex* – the law takes no account of trifling matters. It means, for example, that there should not be a prosecution for theft of five pence or litigation over an order for 700 apples, two of which arrive at the purchaser bruised. It is difficult to see, however, how that might apply in the Subway case, as even an inch can become important where it is one-twelfth of a product.

Application of the *de minimis* principle has produced various odd results. Sometimes, what seem like minimal matters get into court. In 1983, a couple from Kent, England, removed a defective fence post on their land, and after they had repaired it, replaced it two inches further into their neighbour's land. This two-inch dispute, however, cranked up into a two-year saga of litigation, and the judgment was so convoluted it took the judge two hours to read.

In Dubai, in 2007, a British citizen, Keith Brown, was sentenced to four years' imprisonment for possession of 0.003 grams of cannabis that was on his shoe and was about the weight of a grain of sand.

In 2006, a defendant was ordered to correct his conduct after being wrong by a considerably smaller proportion than one inch on a 12-inch sandwich. Dietmar Hehenberger, an Austrian hotelier, had to saw off part of his hotel roof because it was overhanging the Czech Republic. The overhang was 12 inches – not a massive incursion into the Czech Republic, as that extends over 30,450 square miles.

Dollars and sense

White Bear Township, a community of 12,000 in Minnesota, is a pleasant town which the civic authority describes as noted for its "culture of preservation". However, in 2013 a question of "societal norms" arose in one case which concerned the intriguing question of whether a person can be convicted for stealing "free samples".

After Erwin Lingitz, a retired laboratory worker, put
an unusual quantity of free samples of luncheon meat into
cellophane produce bags in a Cub Goods supermarket and
tried to leave, he was accused by a security man of being
a shoplifter. When police officers arrived, he resisted, and
was then arrested and charged with theft and disorderly
conduct. In 2010, Mr Lingitz pleaded not guilty to those
charges and they were allowed to stand on the file for a
year. He did not come to the attention of the authorities
during that time so the charges were dropped without
being tested in a court. Mr Lingitz then sued all those
involved in the incident for US$375,000 in damages for
civil liberty violations, negligence and failure to provide
medical care when he was injured while being arrested.
The civil action, brought in a federal court, was resisted
by all the defendants: Supervalu, which owns Cub
Goods, three police officers, the security guard and the
firm which employed him. Mike Siemienas, speaking for
Supervalu, said that "A reasonable person would not fill
two produce bags with 1.4 pounds of deli meat samples
to take out of the store". He counter-alleged that "The
plaintiff violated societal norms and common customer
understanding regarding free sample practices". Mr
Siemienas said the security guard had a "strong belief,
based on direct physical observation, that shoplifting may
have occurred" and that's why he stopped Mr Lingitz.

Mrs Lingitz, who had been waiting in the car while
her husband had gone in the supermarket to pick up a
prescription, later said "Something is either free or it isn't,
you can't arrest somebody for thievery if it is free". In his
civil claim, Mr Lingitz said that as he left the store he was
confronted by the guard, who pinned him against a stack
of water softener salt and that when the police arrived
they slammed him down on the sidewalk as they tried
to handcuff him, and kicked him in the head and ribs.
A photo accompanying the suit showed Mr Lingitz with
two blackened eyes, a gashed nose and a bruised head.
The supermarket, later asked whether it had any rules
limiting how many free samples a customer can take,
stated "We go with the common-sense rule". So, whether
Mr Lingitz will win his civil case hinges on whether the

force used against him was lawful, and that, in turn, depends on whether what he did in allegedly taking too many free samples was a crime, and that depends on "the common-sense rule". Common sense, however, can be an imprecise principle.

There is little authority on this point. Even cases at Lincoln's Inn on the question "how much is too much?" fail to give a precise answer. In 1498, it became an offence for any member to "cut cheese immoderately". Anyone taking more than a moderate slice was fined 4d. What was a "moderate slice" was not defined though one cheese addict was fined three times for his excesses.

Whether the luncheon meat case can be decided using common sense remains to be seen. The lawyers arguing the case, however, will be on familiar ground if they're equipped with abilities suggested by the late Sir John Mortimer QC. He said "No brilliance is needed in the law. Nothing but common sense, and relatively clean finger-nails".

Plucking ridiculous

Many varieties of "false representation" fraud have been prosecuted over the last two centuries. A case in Middlesbrough, however, was the first one to involve plucked pubic hair.

In 2013, Lee Tyers was prosecuted under section 1 of the Fraud Act 2006 after he did not pay for a curry he had eaten at a restaurant because of pubic hairs on his plate. He alleged the hairs had come from kitchen staff but, using CCTV film taken inside the restaurant, the police were able to see that Mr Tyers put his hand down his trousers and extracted the hair from himself before placing them on the plate. Jamal Chowdhury, the restaurant owner, told Teesside Magistrates' Court that Mr Tyers had been a customer for 18 years and already owed him £110 for previous unpaid meals. On the occasion in question, Mr Tyers assured the owner he had the money to pay for meals for himself and his friend. He then ordered two lamb bhunas, pilau rice, naan bread, drinks, a chapatti and a shish kebab. After the pair had finished their meals,

Tyers called over a waiter to complain about hair in his food. Mr Chowdhury said "He showed me his plate and I said 'I gave you a clean plate'. He had eaten everything but then on the side of the plate there was some brown hair. It was separate and not mixed into the food. I took it under the light and showed him it was brown hair and said that all the staff in the restaurant have black hair". After some discussion, the pair left the restaurant without paying the £39.55 bill. Following his arrest two days later, Mr Tyers answered all the questions put to him by police with "no response". He was found guilty of fraud by false representation and was sentenced to 14 days in jail and ordered to pay £39.55 in compensation.

Odd food contamination instances have featured in some major cases. In 2008, Mr Martin Mustapha and his wife saw a dead fly at the bottom of a drinking water bottle, in their home kitchen in Windsor, Ontario. Mr Mustapha became obsessed with the event and its implications for the health of his family. He developed a major depressive disorder, phobia and anxiety that affected his sleep, sex life, business and willingness to take showers. He sued the supplier of the bottle of water for US$341,000 for psychiatric injury. His claim was eventually rejected by the Canadian Supreme Court. The court said Mr Mustapha failed to show that it was foreseeable that "a person of ordinary fortitude" would suffer serious injury from seeing a fly in a bottle of water. The case cost over C$1 million and buzzed in the heads of lawyers, doctors and company directors for six years. It drew the deliberations of 12 senior Canadian judges and over 50,000 person-at-work hours. In law, one should not underestimate the work that can result from one dead fly.

The opiate of the poppy

Seeds of confusion have been found in legal cases before but one example from 2013 features an unusual culprit: the poppy seed.

A woman in Pennsylvania who ate a poppy seed bagel not long before giving birth was mistakenly classified as a drug user and had her baby taken into care. The mother,

Elizabeth Mort, received a settlement of US$143,500 in litigation filed by the American Civil Liberties Union of Pennsylvania against the hospital which tested her and the local authority which took her child into protective custody. Elizabeth Mort was at Jameson Hospital in April 2010 to give birth. A urine sample taken from her tested positive for opiates. That prompted child welfare workers to take her three-day-old baby, Isabella, from her. Ms Mort was not told at the hospital she had tested positive for a prohibited drug, and she first heard the news when child welfare officers of Lawrence County arrived at her home with an emergency protective order and took Isabella from her. Eating poppy seeds before a drug test can yield trace amounts of opiates, like morphine or heroin, and they can be detected by powerful tests. The drug test carried out at Jameson Hospital could detect an amount of opiates six times smaller than the federal standard for drug tests. The Mandatory Guidelines for Federal Workplace Drug Testing Programs state that the limit for confirming a positive test for opiates is 2,000 nanograms per millilitre of blood. Yet the hospital policy was to alert the authorities if the amount was over only 300 nanograms per millilitre of blood. The legal claim said "Elizabeth Mort never imagined that the last thing she ate before giving birth to her daughter – a poppy seed bagel – would lead to the loss of her newborn, but that is exactly what happened …". The claim alleged that setting the 'positive' test threshold as low as it was set allowed natural compounds in poppy seed foods to trigger false positives. The claim also contended that the hospital had failed to exercise proper care as it did not tell Ms Mort she had tested positive, nor did it ask whether she had eaten anything that could have affected the test results. Ms Mort suffered great anxiety and distress as her baby, once taken away, was not returned until five days later, when local officials agreed there was no evidence the mother had used illegal drugs.

Another unusual defence to a positive drug test came in France 2009 when blame fell on a kiss. The French tennis star, Richard Gasquet, tested positive for cocaine but said that he must have absorbed the drug during passionate French kissing with a woman he had met the previous evening. Gasquet said that he met a woman called Pamela at a restaurant while he was in Miami. They struck up a friendship which quickly became romantic as they went on to a bar and then a strip club. He said they exchanged many French kisses "and good ones, too" in his phrase. The following day in a random test at a tennis tournament, Benzoylecgonine, a metabolite of cocaine, was detected in Gasquet. A tribunal of the International Tennis Federation found that Gasquet and Pamela kissed "at least seven times, each kiss lasting about five to ten seconds". Ingrid Bergman once described a kiss as "a trick designed by nature to stop speech when words become superfluous". The kiss gained a new status in this case as a drug delivery system. Mr Gasquet escaped with only a ten-week ban after the tribunal found that, on the balance of probabilities, the cocaine detected in Gasquet's urine sample had entered his system "by means of Pamela's kissing".

Chapter 4

JUDGES

In his essay, *Of Judicature* (1612), Francis Bacon noted "the place of justice is a hallowed place; and therefore not only the Bench, but the foot pace and precincts and purpose thereof ought to be preserved without scandal and corruption". Things, however, don't always work out like that in practice. As Mr Justice Jackson, of the US Supreme Court, noted in 1952, judges "sometimes exhibit vanity, irascibility, narrowness, arrogance and other weaknesses to which human flesh is heir".

It is because of the lofty and austere nature of judges on the Bench that a fall from grace seems particularly shocking and, in some cases, distinctly risible. History has seen judges take bribes, urinate in court, drink port on the Bench, read newspapers while counsel make submissions, fall asleep during cases and punish vengefully.

Judges, more than most people, are exposed to a difficult and vexed flow of the general population. This means that in addition to cases where they themselves slip from perfection, judges are occasionally the victims of various torments from disgruntled litigants, impertinent witnesses and caustic lawyers.

The chapter on judges in the previous book in the series, *More Weird Cases*, contained the case of a judge who stalked lawyers, the Australian judge who triggered a test case when he objected to being called "mate" by a defendant, and a judge who took loaded firearms and a prostitute to the drug deals he made to feed his synthetic heroin and cocaine addiction. Here are some more odd instances of judges falling below the judicial benchmark or suffering the slings and arrows of outrageous forensic fortune.

The pizza order

In court, it is most important for defendants to be polite to the judge.

It is clearly impolite to say to a judge at the beginning of a case "Now listen here, mate, you don't know what you're fucking talking about". It is also improper, when being given an order by a judge, to reply "Stick your trial up your fucking arse".

In a great testament to judicial patience, however, the defendant who made those remarks to Mr Justice Daubney in the Supreme Court of Queensland in 2012 was allowed to vent his full foul-mouthed fury while perfect dignity was maintained by the Bench. The defendant, David Allan Baker, was charged with attempted murder. He was appearing at a preliminary hearing when he aimed a tirade of curses at the judge. The trouble began when the judge explained to Mr Baker that he would have to represent himself as he'd fired his solicitor ("that fucking prick", in Mr Baker's phrase) and, as a result, his barrister had withdrawn. When Mr Baker said he would just get new lawyers, the judge said "No, you tried that last time". Mr Justice Daubney then tried to explain that the main witness for the prosecution was a protected witness and she would be subject to special rules. But the judge wasn't able to explain fully what those rules were because of Mr Baker's constant obscene interruptions. Mr Baker made a highly improper anatomical suggestion, but the judge, showing extraordinary self-restraint, simply explained that the suggestion was impossible:

Defendant: You can stick your fucking trial up your arse.
His Honour: Well, that won't be happening to me.

When the judge attempted to make an order, Mr Baker continued his exercise in studied disrespect:

His Honour: I order …

Defendant: You can order what you like …
His Honour: I order …
Defendant: Order me a fucking pizza while you're at it.

The defendant upgraded his invective as the hearing continued. Moving into a shocking degree of filthy language against the judge, Mr Baker said:

Defendant: No, hey, listen here you fuckin' stupid old cunt, I've got fuckin' paperwork here, if you weren't so pigheaded and using your big fuckin' fat lard arse, you might have fuckin' read it before you fuckin' jumped the gun …

Sending the defendant back to the cells to face trial the following day, Mr Justice Daubney thanked the departing lawyers and said "I was actually called much worse things on the rugby paddock". Mr Baker was later convicted of attempted murder and sentenced to 15 years' imprisonment.

In Queensland, however, it is possible to get in trouble for speaking to a judge in a tone that is too friendly, as opposed to too filthy.

In Ipswich Magistrates' Court in 2010, Thomas John Collins, 35, became the first man in Australian legal history to be jailed for calling the judge "mate". At the outset of the drink-driving case, when answering the magistrate, Matthew McLaughlin, Collins called him "mate" more than once. Mr Collins was put in a court cell after he failed to respond appropriately when challenged over his use of the friendly Australian term of endearment:

Magistrate: I am not "mate"; I'm "sir" or "your honour". Do you understand?
Defendant: Okay, mate.

The blunt bat of Justice Sharp

In a case in Texas in 2012, it was held that a judge had drifted from the niceties of judicial behaviour.

Annoyed with a detention officer who wouldn't release the daughter of his friend, the judge said "If I had had a baseball bat ... that son of a bitch would have been cracked upside the head. Fucking little cocksucker". The utterance was revealed when the State Commission on Judicial Conduct heard the extraordinary case of the Honourable James Patrick Sharp, Jr, Justice on the First Court of Appeals in Houston, Harris County, Texas.

On 17 January 2012, at approximately 8pm, Justice Sharp received a phone call from a family friend informing him that her 15-year-old daughter had been arrested for shoplifting at a department store in Brazoria County. The friend told Justice Sharp that her daughter had been taken to the county juvenile detention centre. She said staff had told her that pursuant to standard policy, her daughter would not be released until the following morning. She asked Justice Sharp for assistance in securing her daughter's early release so that her daughter would not have to spend the night at the facility. The judge then made a bizarre series of calls, throwing his judicial weight about, unsuccessfully, to get the girl released. The detention was perfectly in line with Brazoria County standing policy that required the girl to remain in detention until the following morning, at which time a judge would review her case. But Justice Sharp refused to accept that state of affairs. During a conversation with the assistant director of the detention centre, Justice Sharp referred to the possibility of Brazoria County being sued for failing to release the juvenile that night, stating "[Y] our county is going to be sued for hundreds of thousands of dollars for this. You'll have picked the wrong little girl that has friends in high places to mess with". Justice Sharp also stated to the assistant director "Well, I can tell you this, things are about to change in Brazoria County. You guys are a bunch of backwoods hillbillies that use screwed up methods in dealing with children".

In voicemail and text messages to the local Commissioner, Justice Sharp complained that an officer at the detention centre had been "rude" to him. He said the officer was the "most arrogant little prick" he had ever talked to in his life and that if he had met the officer "in person", the officer would have known that he "had visited". The State Commission on Judicial Conduct found that Justice Sharp "lent the prestige of his judicial office to advance the private interests of his friend and her daughter in wilful and persistent violation of the Texas Code of Judicial Conduct". For his "inappropriate and unseemly extra-judicial behaviour" the judge was issued with a public reprimand.

Cases of inappropriate use of judicial power are rare. In 1980, however, a circuit judge from Milwaukee called Christ T Seraphim was suspended for three years without pay for a catalogue of bullying incidents. The judicial commission found that "his berating and disparagement" of defence counsel and defendants, his use of bail as "an instrument of retaliation" and other egregious errors all evidenced "a temperament unsuited for judicial office".

There are, however, gentler ways of having a judicial swagger, as the momentously influential, law-making judge Lord Denning once demonstrated. As a passenger in his neighbour's car one day, Denning was admonished for not wearing a safety belt. "You know it's the law", his driver advised. With a characteristic chuckle Denning replied "I am the law".

Denuded of gravitas

Judges have been making puns for centuries. In the 17th century, when a defendant threw a rock at Chief Justice Richardson, it missed as the judge momentarily slouched on the Bench but he responded "You see, if I had been an upright judge, I had been slaine".

In a case about strippers in a "gentlemen's club" in San Antonio, Texas in 2013, US District Judge Fred Biery took punning to extraordinary lengths with prolific references to such things as legal cover-ups and the naked truth. The case turned on an ordinance (a local law) which said that if a business wants to run shows with semi-naked women, it must get a special licence and come under close scrutiny from the authorities. Strip clubs which had wanted to evade a previous law, in 2005, dressed their performers in G-strings and 'pasties' (adhesive stickers placed on parts of the breast) and said that such "clothing" allowed the club to be governed by the more genteel "dance hall" licence system. So a new law was passed saying that unless dancers are covered by at least a bikini their employers will be subject to the harsher checks of the adult entertainment world. A strip club called "35 Bar and Grille" challenged the validity of the ordinance, arguing that it breached its First Amendment right to "free expression" by putting an undue control on the artistic expression of dancing like lap dancing. Judge Biery started as he meant to continue by opening his judgment with the line "An ordinance dealing with semi-nude dancers has once again fallen on the Court's lap". He said the plaintiffs (the club owners) "clothe themselves in the First Amendment seeking to provide cover against another alleged naked grab of unconstitutional power". He explained that the plaintiffs, and by extension their customers, "seek an erection of a constitutional wall separating themselves from the regulatory power of government". His honour continued by noting that while, for the plaintiffs "enforcement of the ordinance would strip them of their profits, adversely impacting their bottom line", not to enforce the law would engender increased drug sales and prostitution – phenomena that "need to be girdled more tightly".

Under a sub-heading "To bare, or not to bare, that is the question", the judge noted that these gentlemen's clubs are "nefarious magnets of mischief". Judge Biery observed that this case "exposes the underbelly of America's Romanesque passion for entertainment, sex and money, sought to be covered with constitutional prophylaxis". In one of the oddest passages of *obiter dicta* (judicial musings not essential to the outcome of a case) to be found in the law reports, Judge Biery suggested that visitors to the raunchy club would have better liked the 20th-century San Antonio act of "Miss Wiggles". He said the exotic dancer, who died aged 90 in 2012, was very good and always clothed. Bizarrely, he appended a colour photo of Miss Wiggles, in a leopard skin leotard standing on her head on a stool. In rejecting the plaintiff's case, Judge Biery put an appendix to the judgment with a full case coverage and legal citations "for those interested in a lengthy exposition, those who wish to appeal, and those who suffer from insomnia".

Strip clubs have been addressed under English law. In 1961, Geoffrey Quinn, also known as Paul Raymond, was prosecuted for keeping a disorderly house, a strip club called the Raymond Revuebar, in London. Mr Quinn's counsel tried to get the judge to see the entertainment himself so as best to evaluate its alleged indecency. At one point, counsel even offered to bring the strip show into court but the appearance of a band blasting out "The Stripper" while near-naked ladies twirled their removed garments before throwing them around the courtroom was politely declined by the Bench. Dressed, to borrow from Shakespeare, in more than "a little brief authority", the court convicted Mr Quinn.

I can't come to the phone right now

Judges get understandably irritated when mobile phones ring in court. It doesn't serve justice well if, while counsel or witnesses are speaking in solemn tones, the court is suddenly given a loud ringtone blast of One Direction or the theme tune to *Mission Impossible*.

Ringing phones have sometimes been confiscated by judges, and in one American case, a judge had the whole courtroom effectively put under arrest until the culprit confessed it was his phone which rang.

So, when a cell phone went off in the Minneapolis courtroom of US District Chief Judge Michael Davis in 2011, everyone in court became very anxious. The ringing was loud but it was hard to tell where it was coming from. Various people in court nervously started rummaging through their pockets and bags in search of the offending article. In Minneapolis, court bailiffs have a reputation of zero tolerance for phone ringing and the owners are immediately escorted out of the courtroom. Judge Davis was in the middle of questioning Fawsiyo Farah, who was in court to enter a guilty plea in an identity theft case, when the ringing started. The judge was not impressed. As the ringing went on, however, its source gradually became clear: the offending phone was sitting inside the judge's robes. "I apologise", he announced gravely while trying to get through his robe to the phone. Unfortunately, the courtroom's advanced sound system with a microphone right in front of the judge meant that the phone rings were amplified resoundingly. The judge was not escorted out of the court by bailiffs.

Unusual audio interruptions have stopped some earlier cases. In October 2007, at the Magistrates' Court in Ipswich, Queensland, a standard criminal trial was suddenly disrupted by the sound of a gasping female voice in an evident state of excitement. The sound, coming from the court gallery, was exclaiming "Oh yeah ... yeah ... oh yeah ... do it to me". The pleasure expressed didn't seem to be an appreciation of the way criminal justice was being administered in Queensland. It quickly became clear that her voice was just the ringtone on the phone of a man in the public gallery. As the sounds of ecstasy became progressively louder the court fell into silence, and the man with the extraordinary ringtone fumbled desperately to turn off his phone. He was cautioned for contempt of court but spared any sanction.

In 2007 in England, Paul Fitton took mobile phone manners into a new territory of indifference. He was convicted of contempt because, while standing in the dock facing a criminal hearing at Blackpool Magistrates' Court, he interrupted the district judge to answer his phone and began a conversation with the loud salutation "Hello ... I'm in court".

Courtroom etiquette

In court, there are numerous rules of etiquette that everyone must obey. These include basic dress codes, how to address the judge and how to behave.

Quite high up on that list of conduct is the need to avoid urinating in the judge's waste-paper bin. That, however, is where Corey Webb went wrong in a case in Tyler, Texas in 2011. Webb was on trial for aggravated assault after shooting a police officer at a youth detention centre. The courtroom urination, which occurred during the trial, was caught on CCTV and shows Webb smirking as he unbuckles his belt before walking over to the bin. The judge dealt with the incident with some restraint. He said "I don't know how you were raised, but peeing in a trash can in a state district courtroom is inappropriate behaviour". He then exercised notable patience by saying "This is the second conversation we have had. There won't be a third".

There are some odd precedents of people being convicted for urinating in the wrong place at the wrong time. In 1663, Sir Charles Sedley was fined "2000 mark", sent to prison for a week, and bound over to keep good behaviour for a year after confessing to "shewing himself naked" on a balcony in Covent Garden, London, from where he "piss'd down on the people's heads". In his diary entry for that time, however, Samuel Peyps went a bit further in giving detail that was given in court but omitted from the law report. It was not a straightforward case of urinating on the public. On the balcony, Sedley had "acted all the postures of lust and buggery that could be imagined". He had then "washed his virile member in a glass of wine and swallowed the wine" before drinking the King's health.

One of the most celebrated cases about how theories of "natural justice" apply in English law arose in a case in 1976 about urinating in public. One evening, after Barnsley market had closed, Harry Hook, a market trader, had an urgent call of nature. As the public toilets were locked he went into a side street and, as Lord Denning put it, "there made water, or 'urinated' as it is now said". No one saw the incident except two council officers. Harry Hook was, however, eventually banned from trading in the market and had his trader's licence revoked. Overturning that ban, the Court of Appeal ruled that the council committee which heard Mr Hook's case had acted unfairly by keeping him out of the meeting at key points.

Although urinating in a court room was a bad choice for Corey Webb in Texas in 2011, it wasn't unknown in English courtrooms in the 17th century for judges to urinate in court. In a case in 1848, Chief Baron Pollock said "I remember that in our older Courts of Justice, the judge retired to the corner of the court, for a necessary purpose, even in the presence of ladies".

On one occasion, a law student had emptied some thick black ink into a porcelain vase in the corner of the court. Later, as a legal history volume recounts, the Lord Chief Justice when using the vase "believed himself to be attacked by some mortal disorder".

The swoosh of perverted justice

While presiding at trials, judges should be polite, fair and maintain good decorum. Masturbating using a "penis pump" during trials is not appropriate judicial conduct, so Judge Donald Thompson from Oklahoma was convicted for indecency offences when he did just that. That conviction was in 2006 but subsequently Thompson battled in litigation to get his judicial pension of US$7,789 a month. In 2011 the Supreme Court of Oklahoma ruled that he was not entitled to the pension because repeated acts of masturbation during trials, including a murder trial, violated his judicial oath. The legal saga began in 2004 when a petition was filed against the judge by the state Attorney General. He sought to have the judge, who tried civil and criminal cases in Creek County District, removed for "immodest conduct" and "moral turpitude". Several witnesses reported hearing the noise of the penis pump coming from beneath the robes of Judge Donald Thompson. A court typist, Lisa Foster, testified that she first started hearing a sound "like a blood pressure cuff being pumped up" in September 2000. The petition said Ms Foster saw Judge Thompson masturbate on a number of occasions and during the course of her employment, saw his penis 15–20 times. The petition stated that "On one occasion, Ms Foster saw Judge Thompson holding his penis up and shaving underneath it with a disposable razor while on the bench". The extraordinary events were also witnessed by police officers giving evidence during a murder trial in Judge Thompson's court. The petition explained that one officer heard "a swooshing kind of air, like kind of ch, ch" and saw Judge Thompson "making some movement with his upper body and arms". During an interval in the court proceedings, in August 2003, one officer discovered the pump and photographed it as evidence against the judge. In 2006, the judge was put on trial for four counts of felonious indecent exposure arising from mid-trial masturbation. At one point in Thompson's trial, with special prosecutor Richard Smothermon holding up a penis pump seized from Thompson's chambers, Samuel Dakil, a urologist, described to jurors how the pump works. A clear plastic cylinder is placed over the penis, down to its base, Dr Dakil explained. The other end of the cylinder has an air hose extending to a pump with callipers. When the callipers are depressed, air is drawn away from the cylinder and the vacuum draws blood into the penis, causing it to stiffen. The urologist explained all this to the sound of the prosecutor holding the device and pumping it. Eight former jurors testified to having heard noises like the sounds of a bicycle pump coming from Thompson's Bench throughout the trials. Thompson was convicted and sentenced to four years' imprisonment and a US$40,000 fine. He served 20 months. The Supreme Court of Oklahoma upheld a decision by the Oklahoma Public Employees Retirement System Board of Trustees denying Thompson his judicial pension for violating his judicial oath.

Judges have occasionally been disciplined for inappropriate sexual conduct in court – mostly directed at female lawyers.

In 1993, a judicial inquiry in Canada found the conduct of Judge Walter Hryciuk improper and tantamount to sexual assault, though a later court found that the inquiry hadn't technically complied with procedural law. The judge had made unwanted advances to women, and the plastic panel of the light switch on the wall of his judicial chambers depicted a lawyer with his trousers down. The protruding switch extended from the picture of the man in the place where his penis would be. According to the judicial inquiry, the judge's acts of misconduct included one where he said to a female lawyer as she passed the switch "Ms. Lawson, you can flick my switch anytime".

For sustained sexual indiscretions in court, the prize goes to Judge Warren Doolittle of Nassau District Court in

New York. In 1985, he was given a formal admonishment by the state Commission on Judicial Conduct for a series of inappropriate comments to female attorneys, including telling one she would look great in a bikini and another he would be lenient with her client as she had great legs. One female lawyer was unimpressed by the judge's respect for her legal mind when she walked into the courtroom and was greeted by his unorthodox assessment of her professionalism, "what a set of knockers".

The mother of revenge

In 2012, a mother who came home from work as a state corrections officer in Florida, and found her 19-year-old daughter having consensual sex with a young man, had a strong reaction. She punched him, handcuffed him while he was naked, forced him to kneel, and pointed her gun at him, saying she would kill him if he did not obey her commands. Larry D Butler, the young man in question, sued the officer, Dorethea Collier, and the Sheriff of Palm Beach County. Butler relied on a federal law and argued that Mrs Collier had used "plainly excessive and disproportionate force" to effect an unlawful and unreasonable seizure of him. The decision of the US Court of Appeals for the 11th Circuit reveals the odd drama of the case, and Judge Carnes opens his judgment in an unusual way by adapting the verse of an American singer, Jim Croce:

In one of his ballads, Jim Croce warned that there are four things that you just don't do:

"You don't tug on Superman's cape/ You don't spit into the wind/ You don't pull the mask off that old Lone Ranger/ And you don't mess around with Jim." He could have added a fifth warning to that list: "And you don't let a pistol-packing mother catch you naked in her daughter's closet."

The law report notes "It all started with a phone call". Nineteen-year-old Uzuri Collier called Larry Butler, who was of a similar age, and invited him to her house. That afternoon Mrs Collier returned early and caught them together in an advanced state of romance. Butler had only enough time, the law report says "to dash into the bedroom closet wearing nothing but a look of surprise". The assault to which Butler was then subjected was considerable. At one point, when Butler was crouched naked and with his hands cuffed behind his back, he pleaded with Collier that he could not maintain that position any longer. Collier responded by telling him to bend over or she would shoot him. The legally significant point on which Butler's federal litigation depended was whether, when Mrs Collier subjected him to the ordeal, she was purporting to act in her official capacity – "under colour of law" to use the technical expression. She was, after all, wearing the uniform of the facility where she worked (a youth detention centre) during the assault, and she used her official gun and handcuffs. The appeal court, however, rejected the case of Mr Butler. It ruled that Mrs Collier was not acting officially during the attack. The court noted that, provided they satisfy the right criteria, citizens can possess both guns and handcuffs so Mrs Collier was not enabled to do what she did solely by virtue of her job. It ruled that "any irate mother with an anger management problem could have done what Collier did". The court noted, however, that if the facts alleged in this case were true then what Mrs Collier did was "meaner than a junkyard dog".

It isn't only state corrections officers who have made unorthodox threats. In 1975 in California, the judicial authorities took action against Judge Cannon for her unjudicial conduct. In one instance she ordered a bailiff to bring before her a police officer who had tried to give her a traffic ticket on her way to court. She said to the bailiff "God damn, get that son of a bitch here; find that bastard; I'm not going to start court until that son of a bitch is here". She then elaborated on what fate awaited the officer "When I find him, I'm going to cut off his balls and have them hang over my bench: I'm going to castrate him; I'm going to give him a vasectomy with a .38". Judge Cannon was thrown out of office and she did not get a chance to perform any judicial surgery on the police officer.

The judicial penis

In 2012, the Court of Judicial Discipline in Pennsylvania ruled that a Philadelphia traffic court judge brought his judicial office into disrepute when he showed photos of his penis to a government contractor. Even though judge Willie F Singletary contended that he did not intend to show photographs of his genitals on his phone to a Philadelphia Parking Authority contractor, the Court of Judicial Discipline found that he did mean to show the images. Judge McCune, delivering judgment for the panel of President Judge Curran and a full court, stated "We think that the public – even those members of the public who register the lowest scores on the sensitivity index – do not expect their judges to be conducting photo sessions featuring the judicial penis". One problem for Singletary is that this was not the first time his penis had been the subject of judicial concern. He had been previously suspended by the Court of Common Pleas for showing the images of his genitals to a cashier. Court and Judicial Conduct Board records demonstrated that Singletary showed the photos while he was talking with a cashier and telling her that he would like to go out with her and have an intimate relationship. Singletary, who resigned after he was suspended from his judicial duties, claimed he had completely forgotten about the pictures and that he displayed them inadvertently while showing images of his church and family. Why he had photos of his penis on his phone in the first place was not explained. In one of the oddest passages in a legal ruling, the Court of Judicial Discipline states "We hold that a judge who intentionally grooms his penis for photography, and then intentionally photographs his penis for the purpose of display to others, had better remember that the photographs are in his phone lest they 'slip out' at some inopportune … time".

A psychotic judge

Two problems arise when a judge is acquitted of a crime of violence by a defence of insanity. The first is why was a judge being violent? The second is how can a judge who has been diagnosed with an insanity condition be allowed to continue as a judge?

These questions were triggered by a case in Cook County, Illinois in 2013 where Judge Cynthia Brim was acquitted of battery on a deputy by successfully pleading that she was legally insane at the time of the incident in law offices in Chicago. The court hearing the criminal charge against Judge Brim listened to her attorney argue that at the relevant time the judge was "absolutely psychotic" in the sense of "not having the ability to think straight or to even organize her thinking or to really remember a darn thing that happened". On the day of her arrest, Judge Brim had fallen into a crazed 45-minute rant from the Bench before being involuntarily escorted out of court. The judge, who has been diagnosed with bipolar schizoaffective disorder, sometimes experiences delusions and hallucinations. After the rant episode, the judge decided she wanted to go and complain to the judicial board about a case she had read about in a newspaper. She got lost in the city, however, and walked for five miles before entering the office of a lawyer. She refused to leave for a long time, and then later used physical force against a deputy in a civic building. In answer to Judge Brim's defence lawyers, who said that she was only mentally incapable because she had not taken her medication, the prosecution argued that it was her choice to omit to take her medicine and she must be responsible for the actions which followed. Judge Brim was eventually acquitted of battery because the court decided the issue turned simply on what she knew at the time of the incident, when she was disordered, rather than any earlier fault in not having taken her medicine. Although Judge Brim was suspended from judicial duties after the incident, nine months later she was voted in again as a judge by the Cook County electorate for another six years. It is not clear how much the electorate knew of her background, which included several episodes of bizarre conduct over her 18 years as a judge.

Fortunately, there are very few instances of judges who have been impaired in their work by mental abnormality.

In 2011, however, the case of a US federal judge from Georgia presented some particularly vexed problems. Judge Jack Camp was convicted of a range of serious offences. It turned out he was a regular user of cocaine, marijuana and synthetic heroin, had given a government computer to a prostitute, and had taken two loaded guns to one of his drug deals. The real problem, however, came with the plea of mitigation he advanced to soften his sentence. He attributed all his misconduct to brain damage he had suffered in 2000 when he fell off a bicycle. He claimed he had been brain-damaged for a decade – a decade in which he presided over 3,000 criminal and civil cases. The judge, who had already resigned, was sentenced to 30 days in jail. His lawyer tried to console all litigants and convicts from the previous ten years by arguing that the judicial brain-damage in question allowed the judge to be good at judging cases and sending people to jail, while only adversely affecting his capacity to refrain from things like taking loaded guns to his drug deals.

A snorting indifference to standards

It can be quite difficult for a judge to maintain the standard of what William Blackstone called "a living oracle". Some failures, however, are more significant than others. A judge who punishes convicts for using drugs while being a serious drug addict himself, for example, would be a fair distance from being "a living oracle". Three cases in America from 2013 illustrate this point.

In Pennsylvania, Judge Paul Pozonsky presided over many hundreds of criminal cases for 14 years. After being investigated for having taken into his possession large quantities of drugs from trials in which he was presiding, he retired and was charged with ten offences. Police first became suspicious of Judge Pozonsky in 2011 after he started to order drug evidence to be handed over to him. Some of his requests related to past cases, including one from a year earlier in which he sought 200 grammes of cocaine. When police later investigated, they discovered that the bags of evidence, which themselves contained the plastic "baggies" in which the drugs had been found, had been tampered with. Evidence seals had been broken on some of them. Some of the baggies had been filled with sodium bicarbonate – baking soda – and contained Judge Pozonsky's DNA. Over 14 years, Judge Pozonsky accumulated in his chambers at the Washington County Courthouse many hundreds of grammes of cocaine, along with marijuana and tablets of Suboxone, a drug used to treat opioid addiction. Significant parts of that collection were missing. On one occasion, he ordered all the evidence for a particular case but then quickly returned every item, including cash and a sword, which was not a drug. He faced 15 charges including violation of state ethics law.

Meanwhile, in Missouri, Judge Joseph Christ was found dead in a hunting lodge having evidently overdosed on cocaine, and his friend, Judge Michael Cook, who found him the morning after they had been out to a hunters' banquet, was later arrested outside the home of a drug defendant and charged with possession. Cocaine was found under Judge Christ's body, and the coroner declared the judge died of cocaine intoxication. A drug dealer allegedly sold drugs to both judges. The dealer had previously been charged with cocaine possession but the charges were dismissed by Judge Cook after the dealer completed a 41-day education programme in a "drug school".

There are, across history, occasional cases of judges who were not entirely models of sobriety. The US federal judge, John Pickering, of New Hampshire, was impeached in 1803 on charges which included intoxication on the Bench.

In England in the 1940s, Mr Justice Charles was renowned for smoking in judicial processions and for belching from excessive beer consumption. Other judges were pressured to resign for reasons of "habitual intemperance".

However bad things are now, they're better than they were historically for both the public and judges. In a single year of his reign in the ninth century, King Alfred executed 44 judges for not coming up to standard.

Chapter 5

DEATH AND VIOLENCE

Some people have seen advantages in death. The British Prime Minister, David Lloyd George, once said that "Death is the most convenient time to tax rich people". By contrast, the guitarist Jimi Hendrix said "Once you're dead, you're made for life". In any event, death is a universal feature of life and is, therefore, the subject of much legal attention.

In an often misquoted remark, Mark Twain said "James Ross Clemens, a cousin of mine, was seriously ill two or three weeks ago in London, but is well now. The report of my illness grew out of his illness; the report of my death was an exaggeration" (*New York Journal*, 2 June, 1897). Most reports of death are not exaggerated, of course, and a certain number of the stranger ones feature in law reports.

Whether violence is a naturally inherent behaviour of human beings or a socially produced characteristic is an interesting question. At present, however, there is much of it about and cynics might casually adopt the view of Francis Bacon who said "Even within the most beautiful landscape, in the trees, under the leaves the insects are eating each other; violence is part of life".

In the previous book in the series, *More Weird Cases*, the chapter on this theme included the case of a man who hurled a scaffolding pole through an art gallery window saying it was an act of art, a mafia don indicted for murder who had to borrow clothes from the presiding judge, a rape defendant who tried to use script from *The Hangover* as part of his defence, and a robber who testified, with evidence, that his intended female victim had overpowered him, bound him, chained him to a radiator, force fed him Viagra pills, and sexually assaulted him for three days until he was badly injured.

Here are more unusual cases concerned with the harshest elements of human conduct.

Shooting a shooting

On 9 April 2004, Special Agent Lee Paige of the Drug Enforcement Agency (DEA) was giving an educational presentation to about 50 parents and children at a community centre in Orlando, Florida. At one point, he took out his firearm and declared "I am the only one in the room professional enough, that I know of, to carry this Glock 40". Two seconds later he accidentally shot himself in the thigh. The presentation was being filmed by a parent and the film soon made its way on to YouTube. Mr Paige then sued his employer claiming that someone in the DEA had leaked the video in violation of his right to privacy – a right that was protected by state and federal law. The claim stated that "as a result of the notoriety arising from the disclosure of the videotape, Mr Paige is no longer permitted or able to give educational motivational speeches and presentations". Of course, a sceptic might say that another reason Mr Paige was no longer a suitable person to make public presentations about safety, especially to rooms full of children, was that he had previously shot himself in a roomful of people during a talk about safety. If his name was billed as a safety presenter in future, the public might well opt to be in another neighbourhood that day. Mr Paige, however, clearly didn't want to listen to any sceptics who simplistically blamed him. So he spent eight years in a legal battle to win his case about the YouTube video. The battle ended when the Washington DC federal district court rejected his case. The US Court of Appeals for the DC Circuit ruled that the video clip of the shooting was not a part of the agency's "system of records". The court also ruled that as the community centre and Mr Paige's presentation were open to the public, and the video contained no private facts, there could be no breach of privacy. The court said there's no right to privacy in such a public event when a public officer does something, knowing he is being filmed. If an officer shoots a firearm in a roomful of children, far from it being a private matter, it is a "matter of public concern".

Although there are instances of law officers brandishing firearms that end up in a court, the use of a firearm by *a lawyer* in court is one of the oddest forensic dramas.

The attorney Earl Rogers (1869–1922) is widely noted as the first trial lawyer to make regular use of courtroom props such as scale models, blackboards and charts. In one case, Rogers needed to discredit a witness who had testified that he had seen Rogers' client commit a murder. The witness had repeatedly sworn that even though he had had a gun pointed at him, he hadn't flinched and had witnessed the subsequent killing. During his closing argument, attorney Rogers suddenly got angry, pulled out a Colt .45 and aimed it with a chilling menace at opposing counsel, causing them to freak out and take cover. After the uproar subsided, Rogers calmly told the jury that what they had witnessed was the natural, normal reaction of any person to a threat of death. He discredited the prosecution witness and won the case. Note to novitiate counsel: using or appearing to use firearms in a court of law is now in violation of legal professional codes.

Getting the ear of a priest

Finding a space in a packed car park can bring out the worst in people.

The fury caused when one person thinks another person has taken their space is infamous. It could drive a priest to violence – and in a case in Perth, Australia in 2012, that's exactly what the prosecution alleged to have happened.

Standing in East Perth Magistrates' Court with a black eye, Father Thomas Henry Byrne, 80, faced a charge of grievous bodily harm over a car park fight involving his neighbour, 81-year-old Father Thomas Joseph Cameron Smith. Father Byrne was accused of biting off the ear of

Father Smith during a fight over a parking space. The fist fight raged outside an apartment block, which houses three retired Catholic priests. According to the prosecution, after the brawl had finished Father Byrne told Father Smith to pick up an item up on the ground. Later, after Father Smith had returned to his flat, he discovered that the item he had picked up and put in his pocket was his right ear. Father Smith then wrapped his severed ear in a tea towel and drove to Dianella Medical Centre in Perth. At the centre, staff phoned for an ambulance and alerted police. He was rushed to Perth's Sir Charles Gairdner Hospital where he underwent surgery to reattach his ear. Prosecutor Chris Lawler told the court that Father Byrne did not have a police record but the state had concerns for the safety of the victim if bail was approved. "They live in the same complex but they are both funded by the Catholic church", Mr Lawler told the court. Magistrate Greg Benn imposed strict bail conditions on Father Byrne, including an order for him not to go within 10 metres of Father Smith, nor act in a violent or threatening manner towards him or attempt to communicate with him. Father Byrne later pleaded guilty and was fined AUS$1000.

How people like the unfortunate priest do under cross-examination is often worthy of note as lawyers have not always come off best in such exchanges. In 1872, Serjeant Armstrong, reputed the best cross-examiner at the Irish Bar, suffered an awkward response from an aged Archbishop:

Counsel: Am I wrong in thinking that you are the most influential man, and decidedly the most influential prelate or potentate in the province of Connaught?

Witness: Well, you know, it is in the sense that they would say that you are the very light of the Bar of Ireland, these are children's compliments.

Any attempt in the Perth case to show the court exactly how the ear of Father Smith became detached would have been treated cautiously. In an appeal in 1966, Lord Denning explained that Norbert Rondel, a personal security officer, had admitted taking the hand of a doorman at a party, tearing it in two, and then biting off part of his ear. Denning noted "He said 'it sounds difficult in cold blood, but I can demonstrate it'. We did not accept his offer".

Dead to the world

In medical science it is easy for a living person to prove he is not dead. In law, however, it is not quite so straightforward.

In Ohio, Donald Miller Jr, who was declared dead by a court in 1994, turned up alive and well in 2005 but was told in proceedings in 2013 that it was not legally possible to declare him alive because such declarations could be made under Ohio law only up until three years after a declaration of death. So after 1997, Mr Miller has been roaming the earth as a legal zombie. Judge Allan Davis of Hancock County Probate Court told Mr Miller "I don't know where that leaves you, but you're still deceased as far as the law is concerned". The story began in 1986 when Mr Miller lost his job and became an alcoholic. He drifted away from Ohio to work in Georgia and Florida. He came to owe US$26,000 in child support for his two daughters. His wife, Robin, eventually applied to court for a declaration of his death so that she could get social security benefits for their children. That declaration was made in 1994. In the case in 2013, Mr Miller had applied to the court to be legally revived because he wanted to obtain a social security number and a driving licence. James Hammer, counsel for Ms Miller, opposed Mr Miller's application to be declared alive because if he were legally alive, Ms Miller might have to repay the benefits she has received for her daughters. Ms Miller, a nurse who is not working because of a disability, said she was not trying to be vindictive toward her former husband by keeping him dead. She said she simply could not afford to repay the money. Noting that Ohio law had prevented him from arriving at any conclusion that would resurrect Mr Miller, Judge Davis said the state legislature might feel obliged by this case of the walking dead to change the law. He said he had not ever encountered any case like this one "but I've only been practising for 43 years".

A curiously stark example of nonchalance to death in England was recounted by Robert Megarry QC in 1955. It concerned a solicitor's bill of costs sent to a client whose will had been drafted which read "To attending at your house with codicil for execution by you, but you were dead – 13 shillings and 4 pence".

Killing Edie Britt

An event of scandalous drama that might have been a plot line from the series *Desperate Housewives* was played out in the Los Angeles Superior Court in 2012. The case starred the producer and cast members of *Desperate Housewives*.

Nicollette Sheridan, the English actress who played the seductress Edie Britt in the series, sued the programme makers for wrongful termination of her US$4 million contract. She claimed her character was killed off after she had an altercation with Marc Cherry, the producer, which ended with him punching her on the head. The litigation drama began each day when Ms Sheridan, who was born in Worthing in Sussex, arrived in a black Cadillac and swept into court through the paparazzi. She wept in court when her lawyer made his opening speech, and her testimony was intense. During the evidence, Ms Sheridan was portrayed by those resisting her claim as a tempestuous and unreliable diva. She was said to be regularly late, madly oversensitive and "hugely rude" to staff. Giving evidence, Mr Cherry said Ms Sheridan often failed to learn her lines. He said he was once called to a furious meeting with co-star Teri Hatcher, who complained that Ms Sheridan "only had five or six lines ... and she didn't know any of them!" At the centre of the case was an argument that took place in September 2008, when Ms Sheridan was told a joke line of her character had been cut from a script. She asked Mr Cherry to write a new funny line to replace it. In response, Mr Cherry told the court, he suggested some "stage business" in which Edie Brit would give her husband "a pinch, or a thing [clip] on the head". Mr Cherry said "I was trying to indicate some playful things she could do to exit the room". As Mr Cherry left the stand after his evidence, Ms Sheridan muttered an obscene curse word at him. Ms Sheridan claimed the swipe at her head was a "nice wallop". She said "It was shocking, humiliating, demeaning. It was unfathomable to me that I'd just been hit by my boss". Some months later, Ms Sheridan discovered that Edie Britt was scripted to suffer a fatal electrocution after first being strangled and then escaping from a car crash. Her lawyers termed this exit a "triple homicide", and argued that it indicated that Edie's departure was actuated by animosity. Mr Cherry denied that claim, and said the decision to kill her character was approved by the studio four months before the alleged assault happened. He said it was time for her character to go as "There were only so many husbands she could sleep with". His lawyer argued that under the First Amendment, he had the right to do what he wanted with the fictional character he created for the show. During the trial, jurors were frequently told 48 characters had been killed on the series, and the court was shown a montage of the various character deaths, including fatal beatings, shootings, car crashes and stabbings. This was also the first court case in which scandal in a forthcoming episode was revealed in court. When being questioned in court about whether any other character of the prominence of Edie Britt had been killed off, an executive producer revealed – spoiler alert – that the character Mike Delfino, played by James Fenton, was to be killed in the next episode. A lawyer lightly asked the judge whether she would impose a gagging order on the courtroom journalists, but the judge explained there were no legal grounds for that request. The jury had to decide the simple question of whether Ms Sheridan was put out of work by a decision of unlawful revenge.

Television drama has posed challenges for the courts before. In 1996, the actress, Hunter Tylo, left her prominent part in the serial *The Bold and the Beautiful* and joined *Melrose Place*. However, before any filming started she announced she was pregnant. The character she was to play was then immediately recast. The production

company said she broke her contract by making a
"material change" to her appearance that would prevent
her playing a seductress. The actress sued. Jurors were
shown charts that the producers kept of Ms Tylo's
projected weight gain showing she would weigh 144
pounds by the time to shoot a key bikini scene. Jurors also
saw scenes in which another star of the series, Heather
Locklear, had her baby bump hidden behind furniture
and leopard print sheets. Jurors awarded Ms Tylo US$4.8
million in damages, causing the production company to
remain quiet for longer than a pregnant pause.

From the coffin to the dock

In 2012, two elderly residents of a southern Italian
town managed to break the law by dying.

Giulio Cesare Fava, the mayor of Falciano del Massico,
about 25 miles north of Naples, issued an edict in March
2012, which stated "It is forbidden for residents ... to
go beyond the boundaries of earthly life, to go into the
afterlife". The law prohibiting death follows a dispute
with Carinola, a neighbouring town, which has owned the
old local cemetery since town boundaries were redrawn
in 1964. Falciano became an independent municipality.
However, when the land divisions were recorded in legal
documents, no one realised that Faliciano should have
been allocated a distinct portion of the local cemetery.
The two neighbouring towns disagreed on a planned
expansion of the cemetery site, so Mayor Fava withdrew
from the project and decided to build a new cemetery for
Falciano del Massico's 3,800 residents. Until Falciano del
Massico gains the necessary legal permits, however, and
builds the new final resting place, there is no more room
for anyone else to be buried, hence the law forbidding
residents to die. The mayor in question was a cardiologist
but even he could not enforce the edict he made.
Referring to the town's recent response to his law, he said
"Unfortunately, two elderly citizens disobeyed". A local
priest, Don Valentio Simoniello, described the perpetual
life law as "a challenge" because the local government
"doesn't have the power to limit death".

The notion of dying illegally once produced a curious case in 16th-century England.

Although the law was changed in 1961, suicide used to be a crime in English law. Suicides – the term for the people who commit the offence – were forbidden a Christian burial, and their property was forfeited to the Crown, often pauperising their families. This law produced some agonised legal arguments. The case of *Hales v Petit* (1562) concerned the death of High Court judge, Sir James Hales. Sir James had taken his own life by throwing himself into the River Stour at Canterbury. His property was therefore set to go to the Crown, according to the law, if he had committed a felonious homicide "in his lifetime". Did he, however, commit the felony of suicide "in his lifetime"? Lawyers for his widow and child, who wanted to inherit his estate, put an ingenious argument. They contended that the felony of suicide was only complete upon death and, therefore, that Sir James was not a felon "in his lifetime". The crime was only complete after his lifetime. It took four of the best lawyers in England in 1562 to refute that argument. They said Mr Justice Hales was a felon because the *act which killed him* (throwing himself into the river) was committed in his lifetime. Here is how Mr Justice Brown put it in his judgment, in one of the oddest paragraphs about a judge to appear in any law report:

> Sir James Hales was dead, and how came he to his death? It may be answered by drowning. And who drowned him? Sir James Hales. And when did he drown him? In his life time. So that Sir James Hales being alive caused Sir James Hales to die, and the act of the living man was the death of the dead man.

And with that pirouetting logic, all the late judge's property was taken by the Crown.

Chapter 6

CHILDREN AND ANIMALS

There is an adage in the world of television that one should never work with children or animals. Those who support that idea can call in aid of their argument many hours of film footage in which actors, presenters and interviewees come a cropper by being spontaneously struck or groped by an animal or being given a naïve and over-candid thought by a child on a live broadcast.

It is the unpredictability of children that gives them their enduring charm and challenge for the law. As John Locke once observed "Children are travellers newly arrived in a strange country of which they know nothing". Interacting with the rest of the animal kingdom, *homo sapiens* have always had an ambivalent relationship – gaining great joy from the other species but sometimes an uneasy one – as George Bernard Shaw noted "When a man wants to murder a tiger he calls it a sport; when a tiger wants to murder him, he calls it ferocity".

In the previous book in the series, *More Weird Cases*, the chapter on children and animals contained cases including those deciding whether Garra Rufa fish used to smooth feet by eating dead skin were "any tool or piece of equipment" within Arizona law, whether "bull fear" in a matador constitutes a breach of contract with his employer, and the issues of a defendant in a bicycle negligence case who had trouble understanding her lawyers because she was only four years old. Here are some more unusual cases from the unpredictable branches of life.

Mother's day in court

"Because of their size, parents may be difficult to discipline properly", the writer PJ O'Rourke noted.

In 2011, Steven and Kathryn, the children of Kimberly Garrity, overcame the size difference by waiting until they were grown up themselves then suing their mother for a variety of alleged parental failures. The children were raised in a US$1.5 million home in Barrington Hills, Illinois. Their legal action accused the defendant of "bad mothering" and cited as examples that she failed to take her daughter to a car show, and sent her son a birthday card he didn't like. Other alleged instances of harm included an incident when the mother didn't agree on the amount of money her daughter wanted to spend on a party dress, and a time when she told her obstinate seven-year-old son that if he refused to fasten his seat-belt she would contact the police. The case, which ran for two years, was heard by the First District Appellate Court of Illinois. It began when the children, then aged 20 and 18, sued their mother for US$50,000 for "the intentional and negligent infliction of emotional distress". In the "bad mothering" suit the children were represented by three lawyers including their father, who was divorced from their mother in 1995. The court exhibits included a birthday card Ms Garrity sent to her son. He alleged that the card was "inappropriate" and failed to include any cash or a cheque. On the front of the card is a photo of a range of tomatoes all looking the same with the exception of one that has plastic eyes. The printed message reads "Son I got this birthday card because it's just like you ... different from all the rest!" Inside the card Steven II's mother had written "Have a great day! Love & Hugs, Mom xoxoxo". Ms Garrity's defence stated that the "litany of childish complaints and ingratitude" from the plaintiffs were simply an attempt by her ex-husband to "seek the ultimate revenge" of having her children accuse her of being "an inadequate mother". A trial court in Cook County dismissed the case, ruling that there was nothing "extreme or outrageous" in the mother's conduct and so no evidence of a tort. The appellate court upheld that decision. It noted that the mother's behaviour was sometimes insensitive but wasn't outside "all possible bounds of decency".

In England, the Children Act 1989 permitted children to bring actions against their parents. Alarm about what that could mean was expressed in cartoons like one showing a child suing his parents because he didn't want to be served broccoli. In the event, there have been just a few cases of children suing their parents.

In the United States, however, Lane New, a 16-year-old from Arkansas, went further than a civil action. He reported his mother, Denise, for criminal harassment when she hassled him on his Facebook account. Denise New said that some of the things he had posted on his account "would make a decent parent's eyes pop out". So she waited until he was away from the computer then wrote harsh things about him on his wall, changed his password, and locked him out of his own account. Lane acted as the complainant and pressed charges. His mother was prosecuted, fined US$435, and permitted to see him again only if she attended classes in anger management and parenting.

Snap judgment

The jaws of the law can be merciless. Sometimes, they can be harsher than the jaws of a wild creature.

In Florida, a man who had his hand bitten off in an alligator attack was charged with the criminal offence of "illegally feeding an alligator" in 2012. Wallace Weatherholt, a 63-year-old airboat captain, was giving a family from Indiana a tour of the Everglades in Florida when he was attacked. Witnesses said that Mr Weatherholt tried to get a nine-foot alligator to surface by patting the water and feeding it. The family told investigators he hung a fish over the side of the boat and had his hand at the water's surface when the alligator attacked. Wildlife officers later tracked and "euthanized" the alligator. Mr Weatherholt's hand was found in the alligator's stomach but could not be reattached. Mr Weatherholt was later arrested (without the use of handcuffs), charged with unlawful feeding of the alligator and released on US$1,000 bail. He faced a 60-day jail term and a US$500 fine. There are many alligator attacks each year in Florida in which people are badly injured. The Florida alligator feeding statute was passed to protect people as much as the animals. When alligators, which usually fear humans, become accustomed to human contact they can attack people who do not provide food. However, prosecutors always have the discretion whether to prosecute, and there was no obligation to arrest Mr Weatherholt.

This was not the first time someone has been prosecuted for tangling with a wild creature. The punishment for someone who unlawfully enters a lion's den is usually provided by the lion, not the legal system.

You would think the same thing would be true for someone who enters the Grizzly Bear pit at San Francisco Zoo, but state prosecutors took another approach in 2009. The bear pit is protected by high walls, a barricade, an electrified fence and a deep moat but Kenneth Herron overcame those obstacles and leapt into the pit one afternoon. Herron was eventually snatched from the pit after narrowly escaping being mauled to death. State prosecutors, however, took the view that it would be sensible to have him punished. As Mr Herron clearly had mental issues, and wasn't afraid of jumping into bear pits, what sort of deterrent sentence the prosecutors wanted him to get wasn't obvious. Mr Herron was prosecuted for criminal trespass and "disturbing dangerous animals in a park". The trespass prosecution was rejected by Judge Wallace Douglass. The offence involves entering "and occupying" someone else's property without their consent. The court held that "occupying" means staying for some time and, as Mr Herron didn't stay for a picnic in the pit, the trespass prosecution was ruled to be inappropriate. On the charge of disturbing wild animals in a park, the jury was asked to decide whether the bears were, in fact, disturbed by Mr Herron. Could two 500-pound omnivores be disturbed by a single unarmed man? In looking at who was disturbed in the pit on that day, the court decided it was not the bears.

Putting the goo in a good story

In 2011, a man who sued PepsiCo after he said he found a mouse in a can of its Mountain Dew drink faced an unusual response. The drinks corporation argued that his claim couldn't be true because Mountain Dew contains such acidic flame-retardant chemicals that any mouse in the can would have been reduced to an unrecognisable goo. While the PepsiCo lawyers might have been gleefully anticipating a slam-dunk victory with the assistance of chemical expert testimony, the PepsiCo marketing department were looking less than happy.

Ronald Ball, an oil company worker from Madison County, Illinois, opened a Mountain Dew can from his firm's vending machine in 2009, drank some, tasted something foul and then, when he poured out more drink, discovered a dead mouse. He put the mouse in a Styrofoam cup and displayed it to his co-workers. His lawyer, Samantha Unsell, said her client immediately called Pepsi so the company could stop production on the assembly line. She said a Pepsi representative came to collect the dead mouse. Arguing for a dismissal, PepsiCo cited expert testimony that the mouse would have dissolved in the soda had it been in the can from the time of its bottling until the day the plaintiff drank it. Mountain Dew, it turns out, contains brominated vegetable oil (BVO), an ingredient banned in drinks in Europe and Japan. The oil contains bromine atoms which weigh down the citrus flavouring so it mixes with sugared water instead of floating to the top. The BVO, therefore, gives the canned drink more consistent flavouring. However, BVO is not the sort of thing you would associate with the purity of real mountain dew as it is also added to polystyrene foam cushions in furniture and plastics in electronics to retard chemical reactions that cause fire. The argument advanced by PepsiCo to have the case dismissed said "As Dr. McGill explains, if a mouse is submerged in a fluid with the acidity of Mountain Dew, after 4 to 7 days in the fluid the mouse will have no calcium in its bones and bony structures, the mouse's abdominal structure will rupture, and its cranial cavity (head) is also likely to rupture". The PepsiCo statement went on to say the chemical would eventually cause all of the mouse's structures to disintegrate into a 'jelly-like' substance". The case was finally settled out of court with Mr Ball accepting an undisclosed sum to end the case.

One of the world's most influential cases arose from similar circumstances. On 26 August 1928, May Donoghue sat with a friend in Bethany Café in Paisley, Scotland. The owner brought an order to one table and poured part of an opaque bottle of ginger beer into a tumbler containing ice cream. Mrs Donoghue drank some, and then her friend lifted the bottle to pour the remainder of the ginger beer into the tumbler. It was claimed that the remains of a snail fell out the bottle into the tumbler. Mrs Donoghue was later diagnosed as having gastroenteritis and severe shock. Mrs Donoghue could not sue under contract law since it was her friend, and not she, who had purchased the drink. She, therefore, sued the ginger beer manufacturer alleging negligence. Lord Atkin stated what has become a hallowed legal principle "You must take reasonable care to avoid acts or omissions which you can reasonably foresee would be likely to injure your neighbour". Worldwide, many millions of cases have now been decided on the principle of the snail-in-the-bottle case. The Donoghue case itself, however, was settled for £200 without a trial, so it was never proved that there was actually a snail in the bottle.

No ruff justice

Litigation over the ownership of a cat in 2011 ended because a key witness who was supposed to give evidence, a dog called Hamish, died.

Della Macdonald, in a dispute with another woman about who owned the cat, had planned to call her pet dog, Hamish, as a witness at Stornoway Sheriff Court on the Isle of Lewis. Ms Macdonald claimed that when the court saw the affection the cat showed to Hamish in court, by snuggling up to him, it would be clear that the fought-over feline was hers. The story began in 2010 when Nicola Dempster, a 19-year-old hotel chef from the Western Isles off Scotland, purchased a kitten. She named him Smudge and cared affectionately for him, but after six months he got lost and disappeared. Ms Dempster searched all Smudge's favourite haunts, posted a Facebook appeal and reported him missing to the Cats Protection Society. All of that was, however, to no avail. Meanwhile, Smudge had turned up in a pitiful state outside the door of Della Macdonald. She nourished the black and white stray back to health and named him Oscar. Later, Ms Dempster was euphoric to spot 'Smudge' at a roundabout and took him home. Police were summoned to an explosive altercation when Ms Macdonald discovered where 'Oscar' had been taken. Ms Macdonald's legal action to reclaim 'Oscar' was discontinued as her star witness, Hamish the dog, had died and Ms Macdonald became ill. The judge, Sheriff David Sutherland, decreed that the cat should remain with the original owner, Miss Dempster.

There are odd precedents of cases in which people have disputed the ownership of pets. In 2009 in Florida, two women fought a civil case over a 13-year-old African Grey parrot. For ten years, Angela Colicheski from Florida had loved her parrot Tequila. Then, one day he flew away over her garden fence. Three years later, she was sitting in a local Dunkin Donuts chatting to Sarita Lytell, whom she had just met, when they started to talk about parrots. Lytell said she had one called Lucky that she had found three years earlier. It became evident that he was the one Colicheski had lost but Lytell refused to return him. Tequila didn't give sworn testimony but he did give squawk testimony. As soon as he was brought into court and saw his previous owner he emitted what witnesses said was a loud call of recognition. The court ruled he was the personal property of Ms Colicheski.

Dogs have given testimony in earlier cases. In 1987, a border collie called Tetter appeared in a constructive dismissal case in Hampshire. It became relevant to know whether Tetter, who had been the subject of wrathful outbursts of the employer in the case, was well behaved. Tetter was called to give evidence and responded correctly when given such instructions as "sit" and "up". His evidence assisted the claimant's case.

In 1994, a robbery conviction of two men was secured with the assistance of Ben, an Alsatian tracker dog. On appeal, the Lord Chief Justice said that evidence about a dog's behaviour was admissible provided jurors were warned that "the dog may not always be reliable and cannot be cross-examined".

The 387th most popular name in the United States

From one perspective, a baby's name is one of the least important things about it. As Juliet noted "What's in a name? That which we call a rose/ By any other name would smell as sweet".

A court in Tennessee took a different view in 2013 and ordered that a baby boy named Messiah must, instead, be called Martin. That court's decision, however, was later overruled and the magistrate who renamed the eight-month-old boy was the subject of disciplinary proceedings. Under the relevant Tennessee law, an unmarried mother has the sole right to choose her child's first name. The child's last name must be her last name, her maiden name or a combination of the two surnames. If the father signs a sworn acknowledgment of his paternity then the unmarried mother may give her child the father's surname. In 2012, when Jaleesa Martin and her baby boy's father, Jawaan McCullogh, could not agree on a surname, the matter went to be resolved by magistrate Lu Ann Ballew in Cocke County. The magistrate ordered the boy's surname to be McCullogh, after the father, but she then ventured further and forbade the use of the first name "Messiah". She ruled "This court finds that it is not in the child's best interest to keep the first name, 'Messiah'. 'Messiah' means Saviour, Deliverer, the One who will restore God's Kingdom 'Messiah' is a title held only by Jesus Christ". Magistrate Ballew also said that in a county with a large Christian population "Messiah" could put the boy "at odds with a lot of people". That decision was overruled by Chancellor Telford E Forgety Jr, who declared the lower court had violated the US Constitution, which forbids religious bias in the execution of official duties, and he stated that the court's job was to determine the last name of the child, not his first name. The boy's name is now Messiah DeShawn McCullogh. According to data from the US Social Security Administration, "Messiah" is the 387th most popular name in the US, and "Jesus" is the 101st most popular name. Magistrate Ballew was investigated for religious bias by a panel of the Tennessee Board of Judicial Control and faces a disciplinary charge that alleges she violated the Tennessee judicial code because the messianic status of Jesus is a theological question and not one a judge should prejudge in making a legal decision.

In earlier cases, courts have been challenged by some other unusual names. In 2008, in New Plymouth, New Zealand, a judge ordered that a nine-year-old girl should be renamed as the name her parents had given her was a form of abuse. She was called "Talula Does The Hula From Hawaii".

Other child names that have drawn the parents to court have included Number 16 Bus Shelter, Satan, Hitler, Sex Fruit, 4Real, and for twins, Benson and Hedges, and Fish and Chips.

In 2004, the New Mexico Court of Appeal permitted a man called Snaphappy Fishsuit Mokiligon to change his name to Variable. A few years later, Variable honoured his new name and petitioned for a fresh name change. His new name, however, was seen by the court as a variability too far and the judge ruled it would offend common decency if Variable became "Fuck Censorship!"

Cockatoo blues

The case of Willy, the allegedly cursing cockatoo, and Pharaoh, the provocative cat, came to Warwick Municipal Court in Rhode Island in 2012.

Willy was accused of using foul language against the girlfriend of his owner's ex-husband. Willy is owned by Lynne Taylor and they lived in Harris Avenue. Just yards away lived Craig Fontaine, her ex-husband, his new partner Kathleen Melker, and their cat, Pharaoh. The case against Ms Taylor alleged that Willy squawked profanities, including the phrases "fucking whore" and "fucking slut". Ms Melker believed Ms Taylor trained the bird to use that language against her. Ms Melker posted videos on YouTube documenting the noise. As there is no law governing the use of swear words by birds, Ms Taylor was fined US$15 under a local law controlling noise. That fine was then contested by Ms Taylor. She argued that Willy was provoked by Pharaoh, who kept coming into her yard, and that, in any event, the noise law was unconstitutional and invalid because it was too vague. The vexed relations between the neighbours had already been the subject of other legal orders. Mr Fontaine and Ms Melker obtained restraining orders against Ms Taylor, and Ms Taylor, in turn, took out restraining orders against Ms Melker and her cat. Stephen Peltier, the lawyer representing Ms Taylor, argued that while Willy did make a noise, as could be heard in videos played to the court, it was not too bad and seagulls and wind chimes on the video registered just as loudly. Mr Peltier also denied that the pet bird said "fucking whore". He argued what Willy says might sound like that but was, in reality "knock it off". In an unusual argument for a case with constitutional pretensions, Mr Peltier contended that if you say "Knock it off, knock it off" fast enough in "parrot talk" it sounds like "fucking whore".

Two other over-talkative birds have posed curious legal problems. A parrot called Pepe who used to live in a taxi-cab office in Glasgow was the subject of a legal complaint after being taken to a new home and driving neighbours mad by constantly screeching out taxi bookings. John McAlinden, 55, from Govan was given the yellow-headed Amazon by a friend who told him "he hardly says a word". As soon as Pepe was perched at his new home, however, he started shrieking orders such as "taxi for Govan" and "taxi for Lidl". His all-day repertoire also included "car one" "car two" and "10-4". Strathclyde police listened to Mr McAlinden and to Pepe. They decided not to prosecute and put Pepe on a strict warning.

In a civil case in Argentina in 2006 between Mr Jorge Machado and Mr Rio Vega, Judge Osvaldo Carlos ruled that a parrot called Pepo, which each man claimed was his, should be imprisoned until it uttered the name of its owner. Five days later it squawked "Jorge" and sang the anthem of his beloved football team – San Lorenzo.

This was not the first time a witness has sung like a bird but it was, unlike much parroted testimony, taken to be incontrovertible proof of which side should win the case.

Cat and goat crimes

"Macavity's a Mystery Cat: he's called the Hidden Paw/ For he's a master criminal who can defy the Law". The ability to evade the law shown by TS Eliot's cat was not matched, however, by another feline felon arrested outside a Brazilian prison in 2012.

The cat was just about to enter Judge Luiz de Oliveira Souza Prison in Alagoas, in north east Brazil, when a guard noticed it was walking oddly. The guard recognised the cat as one that often came into the prison and had been raised from a kitten by prisoners. But it looked different. It then tried to evade the guard and a posse was sent to capture it. When it was caught, the cat was found to be wearing a special girdle which contained a variety of saw blades capable of sawing through metal bars, two drill bits for concrete, a cell phone, a memory card, headphones, batteries and a mobile phone charger. The cat was ordered to be detained at a local institution for life, although the judge forbore from the severity of imposing nine life sentences to run consecutively.

Meanwhile, in Sydney, Australia, a goat was acquitted of eating flowers outside the Museum of Contemporary Art. James Dezarnaulds, who travels with a goat called Gary, was issued with an AUS$440 fine after police caught Gary munching on flowers outside the museum. James and Gary regarded this as unjust and after ruminating on the matter, took their case to court. A decision was delivered by magistrate Carolyn Barkell stating that no offence occurred. Magistrate Barkell ruled that the accused goat had been eating the flowers when police arrived. "I accept that he did eat garden plants", she said. There was, however, no evidence Mr Dezarnaulds brought Gary there with the intention of vandalising vegetation. In one of the oddest *obiter dicta* – judicial remarks not necessary for the determination of a case but possibly of help in understanding a decision – the magistrate declared, referring to the Gary the goat, "He may have preferred to have an ice cream". Paul McGirr, lawyer for the goat and his owner, argued that that police had issued the wrong infringement notice because the alleged wrongdoer was a goat whereas the notice related to a person. Mr McGirr also argued that there was no proof that Mr Dezarnaulds was guilty of inciting Gary to eat the flowers. "We can't guess what Gary might have been whispered in his goat ear" he said. The court dismissed the defendant's application for the Crown to pay his legal costs but cancelled his fine. Gary the goat was not required to testify, and left the court, wearing a hat and, modestly, without bleating about his win.

Goats have featured in some other unusual cases. In August 2001, in England, when a Hull-to-Bridlington train made an unscheduled stop in fields, passengers saw an unusual spectacle that caused scores of them to phone the police. Not far from the train Stephen Hall, 23, was having sex with a goat. Mr Hall was later convicted on one count of buggery with an animal. He was sentenced to six months in jail after what must be one of the most optimistic sentencing pleas from a lawyer. Suggesting that a community punishment might be better than custody, Hall's advocate said Hall would be willing also to attend a programme to help him with "victim awareness".

Paw choice of driver

It is not for nothing that the dog is commonly regarded as man's best friend. In one case, a dog saved the life of its critically ill owner in Tumwater, Washington by fetching help, and in another, in Sorgues, France a dog saved its mistress' life by jumping up to stop her from shooting herself.

In Scotland, however, a level of canine heroism more difficult to credit was alleged in court. In a case in 2013, a defendant said that he was not responsible for having driven his car home from a supermarket when he was drunk as he was being chauffeured by his dog. Tain Sheriff Court heard that Ronald Gell, 63, had been shopping in the Co-op store in Alness. He had bought some groceries and a bottle of white rum. The prosecutor, Depute Fiscal Roderick Urquhart, said "It was apparent to the lady at the till he was intoxicated and she became concerned". After he left the store, staff watched as his car pulled away, hitting the kerb. It looked like the driver was drunk so they called the police who drove to Mr Gell's home. When the police arrived, the car was empty. Mr Gell was unpacking shopping. The court was told that when asked to provide the identity of the driver of the vehicle, Mr Gell replied "my dog was driving". The police disputed that suggestion. There was then a confrontation and Mr Gell was arrested. He later admitted assaulting a female police officer by kicking her from the back seat of a police car as she was driving. The judge remanded Mr Gell in custody for background reports.

Man's best friend, the dog, has sometimes come in for tough judicial treatment. In an early English case in 1520, Mr Justice Eliot condemned dogs as "vermin". Over time, the law became more sympathetic but did impose limits. In a Canadian case in 1971, the court was invited to leash canine conduct to the standard of "the reasonable dog".

In a case from Missouri in 1960, a litigant failed to win damages when the hygienic carelessness of his friend's French poodle, called André, ruined his expensive carpet. The court rejected the claim because it turned out that André had been careless on the carpet on more than 75 occasions so the home owner was taken to have acquiesced in the conduct.

In another case, a juror who had a tough bone of contention with trial rules was helped by a thoughtful judge. In 1989, at an Old Bailey robbery trial, the juror became very anxious for his pet Alsatian. He left it one morning to go to court knowing he might be staying in a hotel that night if the jury started to deliberate but did not reach a verdict. That is what happened. The next day, the juror sent a note to Judge Bruce Laughland expressing worry at having to leave his dog for another night. Normally, once jurors have been sent to consider their verdict, they must be kept closetted together, so trips home during their deliberations are not possible. However, having heard the plea about how distressed the dog would be if he didn't see his master, Judge Laughland ordered that when jurors were taken by coach to the hotel for the second night, it should stop at the juror's flat in east London. While his 11 fellows waited in the coach, the juror went to take his dog for a walk. The trial ended the following day. Two men were convicted of attempted robbery, and the juror was warmly appreciative that a kind judge had put a dog before dogma.

Rats on a plane

"Rats on a Plane" might be the title of film sooner or later, but before then it will be the sub-heading in any law book which analyses cases tried in New York in 2013.

A flight attendant sued her former employer after she was accused of smuggling rats on to a plane in her underwear. She says she was then subjected to series of checks and searches that gave her symptoms of post-traumatic shock disorder and "debilitating anxiety". In a claim issued in the federal court in Brooklyn, Louann Giambattista said that the allegations made by three American Airlines colleagues were "patently false" and she sought unspecified damages for the anguish she had suffered since the incident. It was alleged that on an international flight from the Caribbean island of St Martin to Miami, Ms Giambattista took two pet rats on board in her tights and underwear. The pilot, who assisted her out of a vehicle at the airport, says he saw a bulge in her clothing and had sight of "a live pet". Another member of the flight crew says she saw Ms Giambattista take pieces of bread from a bread roll hidden in a cup for the purposes of feeding the rodents. Ms Giambattista, says the roll was for her to eat, and she only hid it in a cup to avoid seeming unprofessional in front of passengers. Her colleagues reported her to the air authorities on landing in Florida and she was, she alleged, then searched and questioned for an hour by Immigration and Customs

Enforcement officials. Although no rats were ever found, Ms Giambattista alleged she remained blacklisted for more than a year, with her passport flagged as someone of concern, and federal agents subjected her to stops and searches every time she passed through customs thereby "making it nearly impossible for [her] to report to work". She claimed she was put "on display" during one interrogation in an employee break room, as other airline employees walked in and out. American Airlines, Ms Giambattista also alleged, declined to transfer her to domestic flights so she could avoid customs. Ms Giambattista's lawyer, who might know more about law than psychiatry, told news media "Everybody has pets – she has her pets at home, not at work. She's not a nut. They're making her out to be a nut".

Rats have appeared before in legal cases – most infamously as defendants in 16th-century France. Around 1510, for eating a barley crop in Autun, a pack of rats was prosecuted. Bartholomew Chassenée, the rats' lawyer, used many adroit arguments on their behalf. He won one adjournment because the trumpets used to summon the rats to court hadn't brought all of them there, and, he argued, no one should be tried in their absence. The court conceded and asked for a better summonsing to court to take place through sermons. Then, when the court tried to start the trial later (with some rats absent), Chassenée asked for a further adjournment. He cited the ancient principle that no defendant was required to risk life or limb in getting to court, and that his rat clients couldn't attend because their route to court was beset with the dangers of cats and dogs. He won another postponement. Eventually, however, the rats got banished – but only after many of them had been able to flee the court's jurisdiction because of their conscientious lawyer. It is not known whether the Town Crier announced the news as "Another lawyer helps dirty rats escape justice".

Chapter 7

There are now one billion cars on the roads of the world. Cars have become so common that in some settings walking looks unnatural. In *A Walk in the Woods: Rediscovering America on the Appalachian Trail*, Bill Bryson noted that, while on foot, "Four times I was honked at for having the temerity to proceed through town without the benefit of metal".

Cars are a major part of the life of common humanity and law courts spend a lot of time dealing with issues generated by this abundant form of vehicular transport. Life on the roads is full of mysteries and generates many types of strong feeling. As the American comic, George Carlin, observed "Have you ever noticed? Anybody going slower than you is an idiot, and anyone going faster than you is a moron".

In the previous book in the series, *More Weird Cases*, the chapter on travel highlighted cases involving a man who raced down a road four times over the alcohol limit and made a rude manual gesture to a driver whom he perilously overtook, only to discover it was the Chief Constable of Durham, a man stopped at an airport with nearly £10,000 in his underpants, and a flight attendant who resigned by taking two beers and then opening the emergency chute sliding into fame and a criminal trespass case. Here are some more unusual cases of mankind in motion.

When a company keeps you company

In 2012, on Highway 101 in Marin County, California, a traffic cop pulled over a car being driven with no passenger in the carpool lane. Driving in the high-occupancy vehicle lane without a passenger carries a US$478 penalty. The driver, Jonathan Frieman, then presented the officer with an unexpected defence. He said he did have a passenger, and pointed to some documents on the front passenger seat. When the officer said there was no person on the seat, Frieman replied that the papers represented his corporation, JoMiJo Foundation, and that as a corporation is a "legal person" it must be seen as being a person in his car. So, he said, he did have a passenger and did not have to pay the penalty.

Since 1819, the US Supreme Court has recognised that a corporation has a distinct legal personality. This means a company can, like a human being, do things such as make contracts and have bank accounts.

The question of how far a corporation is a "legal person" has flared as a political issue in recent times in America. In 2010, in *Citizens United v Federal Election Commission*, the Supreme Court decided that to restrict the money corporations can give to political parties or politicians would amount to a violation of companies' First Amendment rights to free speech. Some commentators have argued that it, therefore, follows from the Supreme Court decision that the Constitution affords protections to corporations as if they were people.

Ford Greene, the lawyer representing Jonathan Frieman in the carpool lane case, argued that the state vehicle code treated a corporation as equivalent to a real person so the company could be seen as a passenger. Vehicle Code section 470 defines a "person" as "a natural person, firm ... limited liability company, or corporation". Mr Greene argued that "When a corporation is present in one's car, it is sufficient to qualify as a two-person occupancy for commuter lane purposes". Referring indirectly to the Supreme Court decision in 2010, he also said "When the corporate presence in our electoral process is financially dominant, by parity it appears appropriate to recognise such presence in an automobile". Observing that the purpose of the carpool lane law is to reduce traffic congestion, the court ruled that sharing a ride with corporate documents did not serve that purpose. Mr Frieman was ordered to pay the US$478 penalty.

Police officers who stop cars which are breaking the law have been given some unusual excuses in other jurisdictions.

Omed Aziz was stopped by traffic police in April 2006 in the West Midlands for dangerous driving. A police officer described how, after pulling Mr Aziz over for driving on the wrong side of the road, he asked him to remove his sunglasses. In court, the prosecuting lawyer asked the officer if he had noticed anything in particular when Aziz removed his shades. The officer replied "I did – he didn't have any eyes". "I attempted to speak to the driver, who appeared to be fumbling around with the controls", the officer said. "At that point the passenger leaned across and stated, 'He's blind'". Mr Aziz was, he said, receiving instructions on how to drive from his passenger. He was convicted of dangerous driving. Justice is blind but does not permit drivers to be so.

Plates of weed

In 2011, an American lawyer argued that freedom of expression extended to licence plates should be as relaxed as possible.

Frank Shoemaker, an attorney from Holbrook, Nebraska, was the sponsor of a petition for a state ballot on the legalisation of marijuana. Mr Shoemaker requested a car licence plate reading "NE 420", letters and numerals that refer to "Nebraska" and "April 20", the date of the unofficial holiday known as "National Pot Smoking Day". The director of the Nebraska Department of Motor Vehicles (DMV), Beverly Neth, refused to issue the licence plate saying that the "420" numerals were sought to promote marijuana use. The American Civil Liberties Union (ACLU) sued the DMV for refusing to issue the personalised plate, arguing that the refusal violated the principle of free speech. Ms Neth, who had clearly done some research into the apparently mundane designation "NE 420" said that it could also be associated with Adolf Hitler, who was born on April 20, 1889 and the Columbine High School massacre in Colorado, which took place on April 20, 1999. The legal director of Nebraska ACLU, Amy Miller, commented that there is nothing obscene or offensive about "NE 420". She said that the proposed licence plate is "purely political speech" relating to the legislative proposal to legalise cannabis. It is unlawful to possess or use marijuana in Nebraska but it isn't unlawful to suggest that marijuana be made legal.

There was a precedent for declining allegedly offensive licences. In 1994, the US District Court in the Eastern District of Virginia ruled such refusals were lawful but, on a legal technicality, it allowed a driver to retain the plate GOVT SUX.

The right to controversial plates has, however, been fully upheld in a more recent case about speciality licence plates – plates with a general message which many people can use alongside their vehicle number.

In the "NE 420" case, the Attorney General of Nebraska, Jon Bruning, upon learning of the lawsuit, advised the DMV to issue the plate, as he believed the courts would rule in the plaintiff's favour. Mr Shoemaker won his plate within one week. In 2009, the 8th US Circuit Court of Appeals ruled that the Missouri Department of Revenue (MDR) couldn't reject an application for a speciality licence plate "CHOOSE LIFE" just because the words represented an organisation's viewpoint, as that would amount to an unconstitutional violation of the right to free speech.

The boundaries of law in many democratic countries allow citizens to shock other people. In general, there's no law against causing offence to others. The late English lawyer, Sir John Mortimer, said "I think causing offence is important and beneficial to humanity. People should be offended three times a week and twice on Sundays".

In the 2009 US case, an anti-abortion group had applied for the "CHOOSE LIFE" licence plate. The MDR said it wouldn't issue the plate because that would amount to a governmental endorsement of a political opinion, but the appeal court granted an order that the plate must be issued. The court said a licence plate was an expression of *personal* opinion, like bumper stickers, and protected by the law of free speech.

Sometimes, the authorities have to think hard and suspiciously about why someone is applying for a particular licence. An application in Alaska for the plate "6CENTS" caused much consternation among officials. They eventually approved it, however, when they focused on the applicant's name: Penny Nickels.

The application for "3M 3TIB" caused some worry. Can you see the difficulty? Do not read on until you've had a go at divining its significance. It was declined permission under the old, stricter law because if the vehicle approached you from behind, what you'd see in your rear view mirror would be "BITE ME".

Driving justice round the bend

Ever since Walter Arnold became the first person to be convicted of speeding for driving at 8mph in Kent, England, in 1896, people's opposition to speeding fines has produced some odd court cases.

The speeding ticket given to Steven Osgood in Cairns, Australia, ended up being the most expensive in history. From having faced an AUS$250 ticket, Osgood became liable for an AUS$10,000 bill after a five-year, very slow journey through the courts. Mr Osgood, 54, lost his final appeal against the AUS$250 penalty in the Supreme Court in Brisbane and was ordered to pay police costs of AUS$10,000. In 2006, a fixed radar on a police car clocked Osgood driving at 93km/h in an 80km/h zone on the highway near Kuranda. Osgood contested the charge, saying the radar's accuracy was to be doubted because the police car was coming over the crest of a hill and around a bend. Mr Osgood took the matter to trial at Cairns Magistrates' Court in 2008. It lasted three days with both he and the police calling expert witnesses. After hearing the evidence, a Cairns magistrate convicted him of speeding and fined him AUS$250 as well as an additional AUS$65 in court costs and AUS$7,209 in prosecution costs. In 2009, Osgood lost an appeal against those costs in Cairns District Court and was ordered to pay another AUS$1,800. Mr Osgood then went to the Court of Appeal in 2012, where he represented himself in court via video link. He claimed there were shortcomings in the use of police radars. He claimed the court's acceptance of the accuracy of the radar device was "biased" and claimed his appeal ought to be heard before a specialist court not presided over by judges, but technically qualified people. In her judgment, Judge Margaret White rejected Mr Osgood's case, refused to grant leave for a further appeal and ordered Osgood to pay the prosecution's costs. The court ruled that "Mr Osgood has not demonstrated any flaw in the approach or failure to understand the scientific evidence adduced". It also noted "No issue of public policy about the accuracy of the devices used by police to detect breaches of the speed limits on Queensland roads is raised on the evidence which would suggest that leave to appeal ought to be granted".

Other jurisdictions have seen some odd attempts to challenge police speed radar evidence.

In 2006, Craig Moore was convicted at Manchester Crown Court in England of blowing up a roadside speed camera. He was sentenced to four months' imprisonment. Having been photographed speeding, he had returned to the scene with industrial explosives to destroy the evidence in the yellow camera box. He had been caught because the explosion triggered the camera to take another photograph which included his vehicle by the scene.

Vikki Fielden appealed at Bradford Crown Court against a speeding conviction in 2008, arguing that the camera which clocked her at 36mph in a 30mph zone was inaccurate as she was travelling on a bend. The theoretical physics used in court, including the arguments of her husband, a university science researcher, didn't prevail and her conviction was upheld.

The first person in America to be convicted of a speeding offence was a taxi-cab driver. For driving at 12mph on Lexington Avenue, Manhattan, on 20 May 1899, Jacob German was arrested. He was working as a taxi-cab driver for the Electric Vehicle Company when he was pulled over. History doesn't record whether the taxi-cab driver narrowed his eyes at the officer and asked "Are you talking to me?".

Dirty money

It pays to give to charity. Unless you are in Cleveland, Ohio in which case it might cost you dearly. When John Davis threw some dollar bills to a beggar he was charged with a littering offence. In 2012, Mr Davis was in his car, leaving a motorway, when he saw the beggar in a wheelchair. He decided, he said, to try to help someone less fortunate than himself and grabbed a few dollars from his wallet. "I have a brother that's paralysed", he said. "My brother's in that same situation and struggles". As he drove towards the man, Mr Davis rolled up the money and extended his arm out of his car window. Mr Davis says the man took the cash but one of the dollars fell to the ground. The man bent over and picked it up. Seconds later, the Ohio Police Department swung into action. Mr Davis was pulled over by a police officer who issued him a penalty for "littering from a moving vehicle". The offence was recorded as "throw paper out window" and in parenthesis "money to panhandler". A panhandler, from "panhandle" a 19th-century word for "an extended forearm", is a beggar. Mr Davis faced a penalty and costs of up to US$500.

The golden award for penal zeal in the field of litter enforcement, however, must go to PC Stuart Gray. In 2009, PC Gray was walking down Newmarket Street in Ayr. Also walking in that street was Stuart Smith, an unemployed man who was living on £49 a week. While walking, Mr Smith accidentally dropped a £10 note from his pocket on to the pavement. Seeing the incident, PC Gray picked up the £10 note and returned it to Mr Smith who thanked him profusely. Mr Smith was then flabbergasted when the officer took out his note book, charged him with littering, and issued him with a £50 penalty. In his police force, PC Gray is nicknamed "Shiny Buttons" because of his keen attention to detail. That isn't, however, how he's referred to now by some people he passes on his beat.

Walk on the crime side

Worldwide, there are about 15,000 different types of criminal offence. In Houston, Texas in 2012, Natalie Plummer was charged with one of the more obscure offences: "walking in the roadway where there is a sidewalk present". In fact, Ms Plummer was arrested after she stood by the side of the road and held aloft a sign alerting drivers to a police speed trap. When riding her bicycle home from a grocery store, Ms Plummer noticed police officers pulling over speeding drivers. She parked her bike and made a makeshift sign warning drivers about the "speed trap" ahead. An officer then drove up and arrested her. "I was completely abiding by the law", Plummer said later on television, "I was simply warning citizens of a situation ahead". She argued that she was just trying to get people to stop driving so fast. After being held in jail for 12 hours, Plummer was released on a bail bond. The police didn't explain why it was necessary to detain her in a cell for 12 hours. Ms Plummer's method of alerting drivers to police speed traps might have been unprecedented, but US state laws covering such warnings are decades old. The most common example of drivers warning each other of speed traps, flashing their headlights, is legal in some US states but illegal in others.

In 2011, a driver in England was convicted of a criminal offence for flashing his headlights at oncoming motorists to warn them of a police speed trap ahead. Michael Thompson, 64, believed he was doing his "civic duty" by alerting drivers on the opposite side of a dual carriageway near Grimsby. He said he had previously been involved in an accident when two drivers in front of him braked sharply after seeing a speed trap and although he braked in time, another motorist crashed into the back of his vehicle. Mr Thompson denied wilfully obstructing a policewoman in the execution of her duty but was convicted after a trial at Grimsby Magistrates' Court. He was fined £175 and ordered to pay £250 costs.

An irregularity in the way police use radar guns to carry out car speed checks was investigated by Devon and Cornwall police in 1999. The case concerned police allegedly playing a game called "traffic snooker". The alleged rules are simple. Motorway traffic police stop speeding cars, scoring as if the cars were snooker balls. So, stopping a red car would score one point, a black car will score seven, followed by another red, and so on until all the colours have been "potted". The officer with the highest "break", a sequence of points, wins. In another version of the alleged game, instead of scoring the appropriate score for the car's colour, traffic officers score the number of points by which the driver's licence will be endorsed. The game came to light following a complaint from a publisher, John Emslie, who was stopped speeding in a yellow Alfa Romeo Spider on the M5. Mr Emslie said that when he asked why his partner, who was driving a black Jeep Cherokee behind him at the same speed, had not been stopped, the officer replied that a game of motorway snooker was in progress. The officer said he and his fellow officers were playing traffic snooker as a way of relieving the boredom of their job, and that the unlucky driver happened to have been speeding in a yellow car – the colour at that moment required to be pocketed by the officer. Pot luck.

Easy rider

High-speed getaways create considerable danger. For example, although they were eventually caught and sent to prison, a criminal gang managed to evade West Midlands police pursuit cars, and even a police helicopter, by driving at 180mph in an Audi RS5 fitted with a Lamborghini engine and racing brakes.

In an altogether different case in 2013, James Phillips showed he was a less cunning criminal, and that is why as part of his sentence at Bristol Crown Court he was ordered to go on a "thinking skills" course. Mr Phillips, a disqualified driver, tried to out-race police pursuit cars and a police helicopter while riding his 50cc moped at 15mph through a Bristol suburb. The drama began when, according to the account given by his counsel in court, police tried to stop Mr Phillips. He panicked and rode away on his 50cc Piaggio scooter. With two powerful cars in pursuit, Mr Phillips phutted along roads and mounted pavements in order to try to escape capture. A video of the event filmed from the police helicopter was played in court. At one point, an officer in the helicopter flying overhead and tracking Phillips' journey is heard to say "Speed is fifteen, one-five, miles an hour". The chase lasted for over a mile while Mr Phillips tootled along, slowing down for speed bumps, with the police cars driving a safe distance behind with flashing lights and sirens blaring. Mr Phillips, 22, pleaded guilty to driving while disqualified and without insurance, and to dangerous driving. He had a previous conviction for dangerous driving after he drove a car from a burglary, from which others hurled bottles at police. For the latest offence he was given a nine-month jail term suspended for 18 months, and ordered to do 100 hours of unpaid work. He was also ordered to undergo a thinking skills programme. He was disqualified from driving for three years, ordered to take an extended driving test and to pay a victim surcharge of £100.

An earlier case involving an extraordinary vehicular traffic violation occurred in Germany in 2007. Guenther Eichmann, 54, was stopped by police in the high street in Geseke for driving at 40mph – twice the speed limit. His case resulted in a £300 fine and the confiscation of his vehicle. But if you examined the prosecution papers, expecting to see that he was driving a Subaru Impreza or a Ferrari then you would be surprised. The vehicle the police had to race to catch was a supercharged and modified electric wheelchair. Mr Eichmann, a former engineer, had modified the wheelchair himself.

The pioneer of the petrol-engine car, Walter Arnold, was the first person in Britain to be fined for speeding. On 27 January 1896, when there were only 20 cars in Britain, Mr Arnold was driving through Paddock Wood in Kent. He was travelling at 8mph – four times over the 2mph limit imposed for built-up areas by the Locomotive Act 1865. A policeman eating his lunch in a nearby cottage abandoned his meal, donned his helmet, and chased the car for some distance on a bicycle before catching Mr Arnold. The fine was one shilling.

Some cases of speeding in Britain have been odd in respect of both the vehicle and the venue. In May 2007, people were having a relaxing game of golf at the Royal Dornoch golf course in Scotland when racing across the 15th fairway towards them came what was reported as "a madman on a horse". There was much alarm and distress. Even the horse was anxious. An accident was narrowly avoided, and Maurice Murphy, 27, was reigned in with a conviction for the old offence of "riding a horse furiously".

Chapter 8

Lawyers

When it comes to social adulation, lawyers aren't widely seen as superheroes. Some lawyers, however, do make it to positions of great renown. Such rises can occur in political life and provide us with such examples as Bill and Hillary Clinton, Margaret Thatcher and Tony Blair. Other fields of endeavour in which lawyers become popular include television, with examples such as Jerry Springer, and Hollywood, with examples such as Gerard Butler. Some lawyers even get glowing reputations for their entertaining legal work. The famed New York trial lawyer, Moe Levine, was reputed to be so good at advocacy that he enjoyed a parallel income from selling tapes of his final arguments.

Some legal practice concerns "non-contentious work" where there are no oppositional sides, such as will-drafting. The courts, however, by definition, deal with disputes. These are disputes in fields such as civil, commercial, family and criminal law. The atmosphere is often very fraught, so tension-breaking moments play to great relief in exchanges like these:

Counsel: I trust I'm not taking too long on this, m'lord. I saw your lordship check the time on your watch.

Judge: I wasn't looking at the time, I was looking at the date.

...

19th-century London

| Counsel: | The doctor will testify to the kleptomania, which I'm sure your lordship understands. |
| Judge: | Yes, it's what I'm here to cure. |

...

| Counsel: | So, just ten days after the car accident you saw yourself as fit enough to return to work at the university as the Dean of the Business School? |
| Witness: | Yes, that's right, doctors X-rayed my head, and found nothing. |

...

19th-century London cross-examination

| Counsel: | Sir, I must say that you have contrived to present your case very well. |
| Witness: | Thank you. I'd return the compliment if I was not testifying under oath. |

...

| Counsel: | It's true isn't it that on 7th May last you ran naked through Bolton market singing "God Save the Queen"? |
| Witness: | What was that date again? |

...

| Counsel: | The drug is expensive isn't it? We're talking £250 a gram. |
| Witness: | Lady, if you're paying that you're buying from the wrong guy. |

...

Counsel:	Are you married?
Witness:	Yes.
Counsel:	I see, and what does your husband do?
Witness:	Whatever he's told.

In the previous book in the series, *More Weird Cases*, cases in this chapter included a lawyer who was slated by an appeal court for copying and pasting his arguments from Wikipedia, a lawyer who took action for the right to wear a baseball cap in court, and a lawyer who sued his law firm for making him go to a training event in which he had to sit in a circle of naked men, pass around a wooden phallus, and tell sex stories. Here are some more remarkable examples of life in what is sometimes described as the world's second oldest profession.

Strikingly bad client conduct

The etiquette of how a client should treat his lawyer is fairly straightforward. The customary "please" and "thank you" are always a good idea. It is also advisable at the end of a trial not to punch your lawyer in the face in court as it shows serious disrespect and gives a bad impression to the judge.

One case from 2012 illustrates this point. Lamarcus Williamson, of South Carolina, was sentenced to 15 years for robbery. He was about to be led from the court when, objecting to the quality of his legal representation, he swung both cuffed hands and sucker-punched defence lawyer Dan Hall in the face, knocking him to the ground. "Court is a tense, emotional, tough situation", the attorney said later, "I'm not a good boxer". Mr Williamson, 30, was called back to court the following day for another hearing, this one for contempt. He told the judge "I was upset because the solicitor was trying to incriminate me like I'm some bad guy". That was an odd comment as Mr Williamson had already pleaded guilty to the charges. Judge Michael Nettles said "It is clear your conduct is not governed by rational thought. [Hall] was just there to help you before you hit him with a roundhouse square in the mouth". For the contempt, Judge Nettles added an extra six months to Williamson's sentence.

There are some odd precedents of misconduct in the courtroom.

In 2009, Megumi Ogawa, a lecturer in law, was representing herself in a trial at Brisbane district court, Australia on charges of using a carriage service (the telephone system or internet) to harass and to threaten to kill two court officials. During a long conflict with the court system she had sent 83 emails and made 176 calls to court staff. Unimpressed by the prosecution's case against her, she lowered her trousers and bared her buttocks at the judge. She was given a predictably poor mark for her understanding of legal procedure, jailed for four months for contempt, and six months for her other crimes.

In 2011, in Everett, Washington, the murder trial of Joshua Monson was interrupted when, taking objection to his lawyer's argument, he stabbed him in the neck with a sharpened pencil. The court was cleared as medical aid was summoned. Later in the trial, on another day, proceedings were interrupted again when Monson tried to stab his replacement lawyer in the neck. After that, the queue of lawyers willing to represent Monson shortened considerably. In order to secure a new lawyer for the violent defendant, the judge ruled that for the rest of the trial Monson must have his hands strapped to a special mobile restraining chair – a bit like the one in which Hannibal Lecter was bound but without the face mask.

78 asks an hour

Occasionally, a case arises which begs the question of how someone became a lawyer. In 2013, in Melbourne, a solicitor was ordered to pay AUS$100,000 compensation to his victim in a sexual harassment case after he gave the court a video, as part of his defence evidence, showing himself at work asking an employee for sex 78 times in one hour. The sexual harassment complaint under the Equal Opportunity Act 1995 was brought by a female trainee, "Ms GLS" (Graduate Law Student), against "Mr PLP" (Principal Law Practitioner), the principal of his own firm. The case was heard by the State of Victoria's Civil and Administrative Tribunal. The recordings, Justice Garde stated, "show Mr PLP pressing Ms GLS for sexual intercourse on no less than 78 occasions, and using all of his persuasive powers to achieve this object". Ms GLS repeatedly declined to have sex with him whilst frequently referring to Mr PLP's relationship with his life partner. The complaint related to a period in 2011 when Ms GLS, a mature student, was undertaking practical legal training as part of her study for a Graduate Diploma of Legal Practice. She was originally paid AUS$50 a day, later rising to AUS$100. She had known Mr PLP since 2006 when they had worked together at a law firm where he was a paralegal and she was a secretary. Judging Mr PLP's conduct, the tribunal noted the contents of his secretly made video and sound recordings of events at his office from about 6pm on 4 July 2011. The tribunal condemned Mr PLP for outrageously making the secret recording of an employee. Mr PLP offered the recording because he thought it demonstrated that he was not being offensive or, if he was, that Ms GLS consented to his conduct. One of the many recorded exchanges Mr PLP found challenging to explain included this unusual request made of a trainee lawyer:

MR PLP:	Yeah, I wouldn't mind to fuck you on the table, but
MS GLS:	No. The answer is no.
MR PLP:	You've got to – you've got to – I don't know. It just seems to be a bit of sexual frustration there, anyway
MS GLS:	With who?
MR PLP:	Between us. There just seems to be a bit of a little chemistry.
MS GLS:	No.
MR PLP:	There is and you've got to admit it, there is. At least if I had one fuck, it would be great.
MS GLS:	Not even a chance.

Awarding the victim AUS$100,000 compensation, the tribunal found multifarious wrongdoing by Mr PLP, including persistent uninvited verbal sexual advances, the showing to the complainant of a pornographic video of himself, ogling the complainant's breasts accompanied by sexual comment, and the giving of an unwelcome massage.

Having or asking for sex with clients has triggered trouble for lawyers in some earlier cases and has generated certain cynical remarks which suggest, in earthy language, that the client might accept or decline a lawyer's sex requests but, either way, they'll end up getting the same treatment.

Another ribald remark arose from a case in America in 2002. A man was standing trial for a triple murder in Washington state when his lawyer, Theresa Olson, was witnessed having sex with him in an interview room in jail. The defendant was later convicted and his lawyer was suspended for two years. The television presenter Jay Leno said "a lawyer in Seattle is in trouble for having sex in jail with her client who is a murderer. How creepy is that, huh? Sex with a lawyer".

The ostrich is a noble animal

In a case in 1704, when law reporting wasn't very professional, a law report cited to Chief Justice Holt turned out to have omitted a material fact. "See the inconvenience of the scrambling reports" the judge spluttered, "they will make us appear to posterity for a parcel of blockheads".

Since then, law reports have become very reliable and clear. Unlike books for young infants, however, law reports don't carry illustrations. A 2011 report of the US Court of Appeals for the 7th Circuit, though, breaks that tradition. It is the first report I have seen to carry whimsical illustrative photos as part of the judgment. The appeal concerns the legal question of when it's okay for lawyers writing their arguments to ignore an apparently relevant precedent if it goes against what they want to contend, and not even refer to it. The US appeal court ruled they can't do that as it would amount to counsel burying their heads in the sand. The report contains two colour photos: one of an ostrich with its head buried in the sand, and another of a suited man on his knees sticking his head in the sand.

Two cases were taken together by the appeal court – one concerned a car accident in Mexico, the other contaminated blood products in Israel. Lawyers for the plaintiffs in both cases wanted US trials but had ignored a precedent-setting judgment from 2009, *Abad v Bayer Corp*, which mandated the transfer of certain types of case to courts abroad. Justice Posner said that if counsel is faced with a precedent which decides the law in a way which goes against his client's interest, he can urge that the previous case is wrongly decided and should be overruled, or that it should be distinguished from his client's case but he may not simply ignore it. Just above the photo of the ostrich with his head in the ground, Justice Posner says "The ostrich is a noble animal, but not a proper model for an appellate advocate". For zoological accuracy, Justice Posner goes on to note that that ostriches don't really bury their heads in the sand when threatened "don't be fooled by the picture below". However, quoting from a 1987 precedent, he says the "ostrich-like tactic of pretending that potentially dispositive authority against a litigant's contention does not exist is as unprofessional as it is pointless".

Although photos in a children's book-style haven't previously appeared in a court judgment, children's verse *has* been used. In a case from New Hampshire in 2007, US magistrate, James Muirhead, wrote his judgment in the style of Dr Seuss's *Cat in the Hat*. Inexplicably, a prisoner litigant had included a hard-boiled egg as part of his request for a preliminary injunction. Magistrate Muirhead ordered that the egg be destroyed, and set forth his judicial opinion thus:

> No fan I am
> Of the egg at hand.
> Just like no ham
> On the kosher plan.
> This egg will rot
> I kid you not.
> And stink it can
> This egg at hand.
> There will be no eggs at court
> To prove a clog in your aort.
> There will be no eggs accepted.
> Objections all will be rejected.
> From this day forth
> This court will ban
> hard-boiled eggs of any brand.
> And if you should not understand
> The meaning of the ban at hand
> Then you should contact either Dan,
> the Deputy Clerk, or my clerk Jan.
> ... Destroy that egg!
> Today! Today!

Today I say! Without delay!
SO ORDERED (with apologies to Dr Seuss).

Learned friends

In *The Godfather*, Michael Corleone famously observes, about a mafia quarrel "It's not personal, Sonny. It's strictly business".

Similarly, lawyers are supposed never to let opposing counsel irritate them personally, but a case from Kansas shows that they don't always succeed.

When a defence lawyer in a commercial litigation case in 2012 requested a temporary postponement because his wife was due to give birth during the trial, the plaintiff's lawyers opposed the request. In objecting to the defence's motion, and saying they should have been told earlier, the plaintiff's lawyers wrote to the judge about the date they calculated the defendant lawyer and his wife executed the conception. Judge Melgren of the US District Court in Kansas regretted that the plaintiff and defence counsel while trained to handle disputes skilfully and "without emotional rancour" had in fact let it slip into a "lawyers' spat". Quoting *The Taming of the Shrew*, the judge said that the standard was for adversaries in the law to "strive mightily, but eat and drink as friends". The defendants had sought the postponement as one of their counsel, Bryan Erman, along with his wife, was expecting their first child just one month into what would be a trial lasting several months. The judge dryly stated that "Given the proposed length of trial and the famous disregard that newborns (especially first-borns) have for such schedules, and given that the trial is scheduled in Kansas City while the new Erman's arrival is scheduled in Dallas", the defendant's request was reasonable. The plaintiff lawyers had gone to elaborate lengths to argue that Mr Erman should have told them many weeks before he did. The judge, however, stated that "For reasons of good taste which should be (though, apparently, are not) too obvious to explain, the Court declines to accept Plaintiffs' invitation to speculate on the time of conception of the Ermans' child". The judge allowed the defendant's motion for a postponement and rebuked the plaintiff's lawyers for their lack of sensitivity. The case report carries the remarkable conclusion "Defendant's Motion is GRANTED. The Ermans are CONGRATULATED".

Giving birth has affected many legal issues, but one case where it did not sway things was the law final examinations of Antonella Magnani from Arezzo, Italy in 2003. Having been told by the authorities that "giving birth" was not an acceptable excuse for her to miss her exams, Mrs Magnani decided to face a panel of examiners in hospital after her contractions had begun. Such an oral examination has good precedent. Law students were orally examined in legal exercises, readings and moots at the Inns in London from the 1340s, although no candidate then was a pregnant woman. After a robust and sustained interrogation, the examiners in Mrs Magnani's exam passed her with top marks. A few hours later, she gave birth to her baby daughter, Giulia.

One case where an imminent birth became an issue was heard by the Canadian judge Mr Justice Cairns. A juror asked if he could be excused from jury duty.

Juror:	My wife is about to conceive a baby.
Counsel:	Your Honour, I think he means his wife is about to *deliver* a baby.
Judge:	Well, he should be there in either event.

Digital messaging

A man who was aspiring to become a lawyer sued New York City in 2012, claiming it is his constitutional right to flip the finger at police.

Robert Bell, from New Jersey, said that having been unlawfully arrested and locked up for such conduct, his chances of being admitted to "the law school(s) of his choice" have been endangered. After leaving the Slaughtered Lamb Pub on West 4th Street one night, Mr Bell, a 26-year-old financial services recruiter, raised his middle finger for "one to two seconds" to a group of police who had just passed him. Another officer a few paces behind saw Bell's "flippin the bird" gesture and arrested him. When asked why he had made the gesture, Mr Bell replied "Because I don't like cops". Mr Bell was charged with disorderly conduct for making an "obscene gesture" and causing public alarm and annoyance. He pleaded not guilty in October 2011 and the case was dismissed when the charging officer failed to show up at the hearing. Bell then sued the city and the police officers in a federal court. He sought an award of compensatory and punitive damages and his attorney's fees. He admitted making the gesture, and his claim noted "he expressed his dislike and distrust for police officers by raising his middle finger towards them, while their backs were turned". He argued that his rights under various provisions of the American constitution, such as freedom of expression, freedom from false arrest, and freedom from retaliatory prosecution, were violated. Mr Bell had some academic thinking and legal precedent to support his case. At the top of his legal claim, various quotations appeared. One was from a legal journal article from 2008 which stated "Since 1886, the middle finger has evolved into perhaps the most commonly used insulting gesture in the United States". Another quotation was from the case of *Coggin v Texas* (2003) which said "These days, 'the bird' is flying everywhere".

In 2009, David Hackbart sued the city of Pittsburgh in federal court for violating his First Amendment right to free speech when an officer cited him for disorderly conduct after Hackbart gave another driver and then the officer the middle finger. The court decided that Mr Hackbart was "expressing his frustration and anger when he gestured with his middle finger to both the driver behind him and to [the Sergeant]". The court held both gestures were protected expressions under the American constitution and Mr Hackbart won US$50,000 in a settlement with the city. That precedent evidently assisted Mr Bell as he eventually won a US$15,000 settlement from the city authority in 2013.

When lawyers throw javelins

Lawyers do not always speak well of each other. In 1921, Lord Clyde observed that "the rhetorical javelins which opposing counsel employ sometimes overshoot the mark". Even when uttered outside court, sharp words used by one lawyer against another can bring them into a court to decide whether an insult is unlawful.

In a case in Edinburgh in 2013, a leading barrister sued a solicitor for defamation. The defamation is alleged to have occurred during a lecture at Edinburgh University. Herbert Kerrigan QC lodged the action with the Court of Session in Edinburgh against Robin Davidson, a solicitor who works for the Scottish Legal Aid Board (SLAB). The action alleged that while giving a guest lecture at Edinburgh's School of Law, Mr Davidson made a derogatory remark about Kerrigan's integrity. In addition, he was alleged to have told students that the QC wears a toupee and is nicknamed "Two Wigs". Mr Kerrigan also sought damages from SLAB whose management had already offered an apology for the upset caused. The alleged comments were reported to Mr Kerrigan by the relative of a student who attended the lecture. Mr Kerrigan, who also practises in England, was called to the Bar in Scotland in 1970 and took silk in 1992. He is a high-profile lawyer in Scotland and is also an ordained Church of Scotland minister. In 2012, he was the sixth highest legal aid earner in Scotland with fees of £254,200.

Lawyers have moved to protect their reputations in some other unusual circumstances. In Belfast in 1988, two prominent QCs each won £50,000 in libel damages after the *Sunday World* wrongly suggested that they had quarrelled in a bakery over who should get to purchase the last remaining chocolate éclair.

Acrimony between lawyers hasn't always been resolved in the courts using an armoury of precedents. Knuckles have sometimes been the weapons of choice. In his *Lives of the Lord Chancellors*, Robert Heuston recorded that a High Court case presided over by Mr Justice AT Lawrence was disrupted by "an outbreak of fisticuffs" between two King's Counsel "the former of whom had made disparaging remarks about the latter's ancestry".

In 2008, Kathy Brewer Rentas was acting as a defence lawyer in a criminal case in Florida. She had been defending her husband. After losing the case, however, she was charged with assault for shaking the prosecutor's hand so vigorously that she injured the woman's shoulder. Ms Brewer approached Jennifer Keene, the prosecutor, for a handshake and then made the long arm of the law even longer by virtually pulling it from its socket. According to an arrest report, Ms Keene didn't shake Ms Brewer's hand at first "but Brewer insisted that she do so and continued to follow Keene". The report, said Brewer, "forcefully grabbed on to Keene's right hand and squeezed it, pulling Keene toward her", and forcing her off balance. With Keene in hand, "Brewer made an upward, then a quick downward motion and pulled Keene toward the ground". One witness said the arm was almost ripped from its shoulder socket. Lawyers are sometimes good at being disarmingly polite but not quite like that.

Suing your law school

When an American law student was accused by his law school of being too quick to make complaints, he responded quickly. He sued the law school, its dean, its associate dean, the president of the university, the senior vice president and the university itself.

Daniel E Skinner was a law student at Wake Forest University's School of Law in North Carolina in 2013. He was not a happy student. He had a number of complaints about the way his law school was run. In one complaint he alleged that the law school was in violation of its licence from the American Bar Association because it did not provide a proper system of written and recorded complaints. He argued that this, and alleged dishonesty in the way his complaints were treated, meant that the law school's licence should be revoked. After lodging his complaint about the complaints system, he got a letter from Suzanne Reynolds, executive associate dean at the law school. She said that "if people disagree with you,

you appear to assume that those persons are acting in bad faith and you accuse them of fraud and deceit". Mr Skinner then issued proceedings for defamation. Noting he has "two masters degrees in the field of education and teaching", he alleged that the letter from Ms Reynolds, which was seen by other staff, was an attack on his professional judgment "in both education and law". The claim said Ms Reynolds' letter was written with malice and was a statement that tended "to impeach the plaintiff in his trade or profession". He sought unspecified damages in excess of US$10,000. Mr Skinner also sent an email to all faculty members calling for the removal of the dean. In Ms Reynolds' letter, he was told that his email violated the rules of the student handbook but he would not be punished. She added "I do not want our lenience to date to make you think we find such conduct acceptable. It is not". In his defamation claim, Mr Skinner said that admonition was defamatory because it wrongly implied he was a person who could, technically, have been punished. He said the law school dean, university president and other parties were all liable under tort law because they knew, or had reason to know, of the way he was being mistreated.

There are some odd precedents of law students bringing legal actions against their schools.

In 2007, a group of law students at the American Justice School of Law in Paducah, Kentucky filed a US$120 million class action against the school's administration. In an 82-page document, the suit alleged that the dean and others engaged in an unusual catalogue of wrongs including racketeering, conspiracy, theft, wire fraud, mail fraud and extortion. The defendants denied the allegations, the case was settled, and the law school was closed.

In 1965, Dr Carl-Theo Thorne, a law student who had failed his LLB examinations, sued the University of London for negligence for failing to recognise his legal skill. Fortified with self-belief, Dr Thorne did not engage a lawyer but acted for himself. In the Court of Appeal, Lord Justice Diplock noted that "in his statement of claim, the plaintiff sets out a good deal of praise of his ability as a lawyer". Unfortunately, however, Dr Thorne's argument against the university got the law all wrong. He missed vital precedents and tried to use an inappropriate legal process, so his case was rejected as "wholly misconceived". This ranks high among the most rigorous re-marks in law school history.

Chapter 9

Jurors, Friends and Defendants

In the civil and criminal cases in which they are used, juries give just a straightforward verdict, but there is an abundance of foible and common humanity in each jury. One cartoon in the *New Yorker* magazine pictures a jury with its foreman standing and addressing the judge "FOREMAN: We find the defendant guilty on all charges, Your Honour. On the positive side, we really liked his openness and energy".

The American television presenter, Jon Stewart, once said "There is no such thing as an impartial jury because there are no impartial people. There are people that argue on the web for hours about who their favourite character on *Friends* is". Court cases worldwide continue to present opportunities for the eccentric traits of jurors and defendants to be showcased on platforms of great gravitas.

In *The Devil's Dictionary*, Ambrose Bierce provides a definition of note "TRIAL, n. A formal inquiry designed to prove and put upon record the blameless characters of judges, advocates and jurors. In order to effect this purpose it is necessary to supply a contrast in the person of one who is called the defendant …". In the previous book in the series, cases in this chapter included one where a lawyer tried to show a jury what fear meant by putting a hand grenade on the jury box and pulling the pin, a case where a woman used anti-slavery laws to try to stop the local council from ordering her to mow her lawn, and a woman who tried to escape her obligation to attend her

trial for forgery by forging a medical note. Here are some
more cases of humanity in all its remarkable glory.

Tears of a clown

Pretending to be mad to get out of an obligation is
rarely a good option, and that is how it worked out for
Susan Cole.

Summoned as a juror in Denver, Colorado in 2012, Ms
Cole arrived in clown makeup, a T-shirt, a dress skirt and
reindeer socks. She was also wearing hair curlers and two
different shoes. When Judge Ann Mansfield, asked the
entire panel of jurors if anyone had a mental illness, Ms
Cole said she had "mental issues". She said she found it
difficult to get up in the morning. She also said she suffered
from post-traumatic shock disorder (PTSD) following
from some awful events in her past. She was excused
from jury service. It was, however, an awful event in her
future, not in her past, that was going to have a greater
effect on Ms Cole. After getting a judicial excusal from
jury service, Ms Cole went on the local radio and boasted
about her ruse. She called in to a programme as "Char
from Denver". She said to the radio presenter, explaining
her stunt "I didn't want to do jury duty, I had too much
on my platter". Among those listening to the programme,
however, was Judge Mansfield, who recognised the
events described. Ms Cole was identified through the
court records and "Char" turned out to be Cole's pen
name. Prosecutors contacted Susan Cole, asking her for
an explanation. Instead of providing the authorities with
a medical certificate confirming her PTSD diagnosis,
however, Ms Cole mysteriously furnished them with a
copy of her book, *Seven Initiations with El-Ways Secrets*.
The book is about using the Bible to deal with "difficult
relationships". It is not clear how the book testifies to the
clinical condition from which she said she suffered. Ms
Cole was charged with the felonies of first-degree perjury
and attempt to influence a public servant (the judge). She
eventually pleaded guilty to attempt to influence a public
servant and second-degree perjury and was sentenced to

a two-year deferred judgment on the felony count, two years of probation and 40 hours of community service.

People offering odd excuses to avoid jury service have rarely been successful.

In 2009, after he rejected a jury summons and was written to again, Erik Slye from Gallatin County, Montana sent another reply saying "Apparently you morons didn't understand me the first time". He said he had better things to do. He said "I would rather count the wrinkles on my dog's balls than sit on a jury. Get it through your thick skulls. Leave me the Fuck alone". This was something of a tactical error on Mr Slye's part because his reply produced the very result he wanted to avoid. He wasn't left alone by the court but, under threat of jail, summoned by the judge to appear and ordered to make a humbling personal apology to all the court officials.

Over time there have been many remarkable excuses offered to courts by prospective jurors who wanted to escape jury duty. These have included one from New Jersey in which a woman wrote "I am a professional psychic so I would know who is guilty even before the trial". That excuse was rejected by the court, but I guess she saw that coming as well.

The prize in the category of international best excuse for being allowed to miss jury duty must go to Mr ACL Blair from London who was called to serve as a juror in 2000. He explained he couldn't afford the time as he was very busy being the Prime Minister.

The law of LOL

The comic, Victor Borge, once observed that "laughter is the shortest distance between two people". A case from India in 2012, however, suggests that laughter can also be the shortest route to court.

Following a legal action by Mr Vinayak Shirsat against a "laughter club", the Mumbai High Court issued an order that daily persistent laughter outside the plaintiff's home must cease. Mr Shirsat, 78, brought an action after suffering "mental agony, pain and nuisance" at his home in suburban Kurla. Every day, members of the "Sheetal

Jogging Association" gathered at 7am to sing and clap for seven minutes. They would roll their heads, swing their arms, circle their hips, stomp their feet, kick, and conclude with very loud relentless laughing for two minutes. To heighten their laughter, club members held their ear lobes, tilted their heads back and stretched their faces wide into smiles. Mr Shirsat's action complained that these "loud and vigorous spells of laughter" were an unlawful nuisance. "They laugh at the top of their voices" his statement complained "every member encourages others to laugh to their heart's content". The purpose of the club is health improvement. Madan Kataria, a doctor, claims to have founded the first laughter yoga club in Mumbai in the 1990s. The therapy is based on the notion that laughter – real or fake – triggers physiological and psychological benefits. Dr Kataria's website says there are now more than 6,000 laughter clubs in 60 countries. In Mr Shirsat's case, Justice SA Bobade stated that "Nobody is asking people to stop laughing. Laughing is not a crime or an offence. It's just that they cannot do it in front of someone else's house creating nuisance. Even laughter can disturb people sometimes".

Laughing was dealt with as a legal matter in the UK in 2009. Stuart Hunt was proceeded against for allegedly "laughing in public". Officers visited his home in Drumnadrochit, near Loch Ness, in Scotland and charged him with laughing at his neighbour's daughter contrary to an anti-social behaviour order (ASBO) imposed on him in 2008. Hunt had fallen into a series of rows with his neighbours, Stuart and Shirley Latham, with whom he shared a private road. The arguments ran for six years. Hunt accused the Lathams of speeding past his house in their car. He then took the law into his own hands by installing speed bumps on the road. That resulted in a £50,000 case at Inverness Sheriff Court which Hunt lost. Following more rows with his neighbours, Hunt was placed under the ASBO whose conditions were nothing if not thorough. Under the court order he was forbidden from staring at people, engaging in slow hand claps at the actions of others, waving objects at people, or laughing at anyone within the jurisdiction of Highlands council. It was the first time someone had been legally ordered not to laugh. Hunt was accused of breaching this ASBO by driving past the Lathams' daughter and laughing at her. He argued he didn't laugh but merely "smiled a bit". He was not convicted.

Urine trouble now

The right not to be filmed when you take a call of nature is protected by law. What, however, if you opt to urinate in your front yard?

A man from France sued Google in 2012 for publishing a photo online on its Street View facility showing him urinating in his front yard. Google Street View enables users of Google Maps to view photos of streets taken by its camera cars, which have cameras held on frames on their roofs. It covers 30 countries and began in France in 2008. The man's claim asserted this exposed him to ridicule and derisive laughter in his rural village in north-west France. The man, who was aged around 50, and lived in a village of about 3,000 people in the Maine-et-Loire region, demanded that his photo be removed by Google. He claimed locals have recognised him despite his face being blurred out. He also sued for infringement of privacy, for having his photo published without his agreement and claimed €10,000 (£8,330) in damages. Google's French lawyer, Christophe Bigot, asked a court in the city of Angers to declare the complaint null and void on the grounds that Google Maps is owned by the company's US headquarters, and not by Google France. The claimant's lawyer, Jean-Noel Bouillard, said "Everyone has the right to a degree of secrecy. In this particular case, it's more amusing than serious. But if he'd been caught kissing a woman other than his wife, he would have had the same issue". The man thought he was hidden from view by his closed gate as he urinated in his front yard. But Google's lens filmed him from above his gate as it passed by. The law suit did not explain why the man was urinating in his front yard.

Regrets, I've had a few

Many authorities have been cited to the Bench at Perth Sheriff Court over the decades, but new ground was broken in 2013 when the defence argument closed with a Frank Sinatra song being belted out in open court.

Jeronimo Bouceiro, representing himself in a case in which he was accused of stalking, sang "I Did it My Way" and the court fell into a stunned silence. Mr Bouceiro was accused of stalking Constable Gillian Farnington, his former landlady, from May 2011 until March 2012, causing her fear and alarm by repeatedly contacting her with texts, emails, phone calls and letters, telling her that he was in love with her and that he was watching her. He even once turned up 2,000 miles from her home while she was on holiday with her child in Turkey. The court heard how a series of progressively bizarre incidents began when Mr Bouceiro became Ms Farnington's lodger at her farmhouse in Errol, Perthshire. Ms Farnington said she asked Bouceiro to leave just a few weeks after he moved in because of his weird behaviour, which included over-feeding her cats, and delivering rants about recycling and her parenting. Constable Farnington said she was shaken when Bouceiro turned up in her hotel in Turkey. She had not told him where she was going on holiday so assumed he had snooped through private papers at her home to discover where she had gone. In her hotel room, Ms Farnington found a note from Bouceiro and a jewellery box containing, mysteriously, a single peanut. After that, she said, he stalked her around the hotel. The basis of Mr Bouceiro's defence was that it was Ms Farnington who had started pestering him for sex at her farm after taking a shine to his lemons and loungewear. He said he was being prosecuted as part of a wider police conspiracy against him. He said that before moving into Ms Farnington's home, he had driven from his Portuguese home with fruit from his garden. He said "An hour after moving in, I took a shower and was really comfortable with my slippers on my feet. I had my loungewear on. I told her I had brought lemons from Portugal and was making my own lemonade". Mr Bouceiro testified "She said 'Oh, that's fantastic.' She started being nice, but was a bit too nice. I don't know what the idea was behind it … I was an innocent guy, a nice guy. She became interested and started harassing me for sex". In closing his case, Mr Bouceiro asked the judge to find him not guilty, then sang from the Sinatra song "For what is a man, what has he got?/ If not himself, then he has naught/ To say the things he truly feels and not the words of one who kneels/ The record shows, I took the blows, and did it my way". Jeronimo Bouceiro was found guilty of stalking Ms Farnington and detained for psychiatric assessment.

Exuberance at the end of a case has sometimes been treated severely by the courts. In Durham Crown Court in 1981, a man who had been acquitted by a jury after spending five months in jail threw up his arms in relief. The judge, regarding this as an insolent contempt of court, immediately sent the man back to jail for the weekend.

Live music has featured very little in court trials. One case where it did was in London in 1963. Copyright owners of the song "In a Little Spanish Town" sued the owners of the song "Why" for breach of copyright. Both songs were played on a piano to the Court of Appeal, which rejected the breach of copyright claim – a decision which was music to the ears of the defendant.

Just a number

The actress, Joan Collins, once remarked that "Age is just a number. It's totally irrelevant unless, of course, you happen to be a bottle of wine".

A case in America in 2011 determined whether an actress has a legal right to keep her age secret. The actress sued Amazon.com in a federal case in Seattle for US$1 million for revealing her age on its Internet Movie Database (IMDb) website and for declining to remove the reference when asked. The actress wasn't named in the litigation – her anonymity was protected by the litigation name 'Jane Doe'. The papers disclosed only that she lives in Texas, is of Asian descent and has an "Americanized stage name". Jane Doe accused IMDb of misusing her personal information after she signed up for the special professional film industry service IMDbPro in 2008. Not long after, she noticed that her date of birth had been added to her public acting profile. She requested that it be removed but IMDb refused. The legal claim states that "If one is perceived to be 'over-the-hill,' i.e., approaching 40, it is nearly impossible for an up-and-coming actress, such as the plaintiff, to get work as she is thought to have less of an 'upside,' therefore, casting directors, producers, directors, agents ... etc. do not give her the same opportunities, regardless of her appearance or talent". So, the writ argued, she lost opportunities for roles younger than her age because of her paper age, but she also missed work which would usually go to someone of her real age because of her youthful appearance. The writ stated the plaintiff has experience of rejection in the film industry for each "40-year-old" role for which she has interviewed because "she does not and cannot physically portray the role of a 40-year-old woman". Amazon and its movie database subsidiary, both based in Seattle, were sued for breach of contract, fraud, and violation of privacy and consumer protection laws. The legal claim sought US$75,000 in compensatory damages and US$1 million in punitive damages. Lawyers for Amazon said the actress was trying to manipulate the federal court system "so she can censor IMDB's display of her birth date and pretend to the world that she is not 40 years old". They said that was "selfish, contrary to the public interest and a frivolous abuse of [the] court's resources". Jane Doe lost her case.

Historically, English law took a less than delicate approach to the age of women. In a case in 1376, in which it was important to know whether a particular woman was of full age, counsel suggested that she be put before the court to determine the answer by inspection. Mr Justice Cavendish replied "There is no man in England who can rightly judge whether she is an infant or of full age, for all women who are thirty years old wish to appear to be eighteen".

Lawyers, however, seem historically to have been challenged in estimating ages of both sexes. In *Lord v Thornton*, a case in Yorkshire in 1616, an advocate argued heroically throughout the case that his client, the defendant, was legally an infant. There was some disagreement about this in court. When, ultimately, church records were consulted to resolve the matter, it turned out that the defendant was not an infant after all. He was 63.

The man who sued his victims

Defining "news", the American journalist, John Bogart, said "If a dog bites a man it is not news, but if a man bites a dog it is".

The test of "legal oddity" was satisfied in a case in 2011 by the application of a similar principle: if kidnap victims sue their kidnapper that isn't odd but if the kidnapper sues his victims it is.

In Kansas, Jesse Dimmick sued the couple he was convicted of kidnapping while on the run from police. In an action for breach of contract, for which he wanted US$235,000 compensation, Dimmick argued that after he ran into Jared and Lindsay Rowley's house in 2009, they reached a legally binding contract that they would hide him in exchange for an unspecified sum of money. Dimmick, who represented himself, stated "[T]he Rowleys reneged on said oral contract, resulting in my being shot in the back by authorities". In a claim filed at Shawnee County District Court, Dimmick noted that "As a result of the plaintiffs breech [sic] of contract, I, the defendant suffered a gunshot to my back, which almost killed me. The hospital bills alone are in excess of $160,000, which I have no way to pay". The drama unfolded in this way. Dimmick, a fugitive facing a murder charge in Colorado, was racing ahead of police in a vehicle chase when police "stop sticks" punctured the tyres of the stolen van he was driving. The van rolled to a stop in the front yard of a newlywed couple: the Rowleys. The Rowleys said that Dimmick burst into their home and confronted them at knifepoint. The couple reportedly gained his trust by eating Cheetos and drinking Dr Pepper with him while watching the Robin Williams' movie, *Patch Adams*. The couple later escaped when Dimmick fell asleep. Police from the city of Topeka said they then entered the house and ordered Dimmick to lie on to his stomach but an officer's rifle accidentally discharged hitting Dimmick in the back. The Rowleys sued Dimmick for trespass and negligent infliction of emotional distress. Dimmick then filed a response seeking to have the Rowleys' claim dismissed and counterclaimed for breach of contract. In his claim, Dimmick said that that after he entered the Rowleys' home, he told them he was "being pursuid [sic] by a person, or persons, who appeared to be police officers, who were trying to kill me". He added "I, the defendant, asked the Rowleys to hide me because I feared for my life. I offered the Rowleys an unspecified amount of money which they agreed upon, therefore forging a legally binding oral contract". The Rowleys resisted his claim on a number of points, including duress and that it's illegal to hide a fugitive so such an agreement would not be legally binding. In the end, Dimmick's civil case was rejected by a judge, and in the criminal courts he was sentenced to 37 years for homicide and 11 years for the kidnapping – sentences to run consecutively.

People have tried to get the courts to enforce some decidedly odd agreements.

In 1924, Lieutenant-Colonel George Parkinson made a £3,000 donation to an ambulance charity having been told by its secretary that for such a sum, he'd be guaranteed a knighthood. When he didn't get a knighthood, he sued to get his cash back. The court rejected his claim explaining you can't legally purchase a knighthood.

Even in modern times some people have some surprising ideas of what money can buy in a contract. In a libel case in 1997, Harrods boss, Mohamed Al Fayed, said he'd been advised MPs could easily be gained for cash. He said he'd paid Neil Hamilton MP. Hamilton then sued for defamation and lost. Mr Al Fayed later elaborated "I could hire these Conservative MPs like hiring taxis off a rank". He said "As far as they were concerned I was 'Profit Mohamed'".

And how do you find Mr Guilty?

If you say to people "I want you *not* to imagine a pink elephant", most of your listeners will fail. In 2012, an unusual appeal decided by the Ontario Court of Appeal in Canada swung on the same principle.

Before the jury were sent out to deliberate in the cocaine-trafficking trial of Prinze Wilson, the judge gave jurors a clear instruction. Madam Justice Faye McWatt told them to respect the presumption of innocence. But she made one little slip. She told the jury the presumption of innocence is only defeated if, and when, "Crown counsel has satisfied you beyond a reasonable doubt that Mr. Guilty – I'm sorry, that Mr. Wilson – is guilty of the crime charged". Mr Wilson was found guilty by the jury but the defence then argued that he did not have a fair trial because the jury would have been affected, even subconsciously, by the judge having referred to him as "Mr Guilty". Mr Wilson's lawyer, Crystal Tomusiak, said "The trial judge erred in failing to order a mistrial or provide a curative instruction after mistakenly referring to the appellant as, 'Mr. Guilty'". Ms Tomusiak argued in a written submission that "The conviction was unreasonable and against the weight of the evidence". Mr Wilson, a 26-year-old industrial firefighter had no previous criminal record. After being convicted of the drug trafficking offence in 2011, and sentenced to almost two years of house arrest, he was dismissed from his job at Ontario Power Generation. Mr. Wilson's appeal failed because the jury were taken by the appeal court to have been capable of seeing the word slip as just that.

Judges have made slips before which appeared to disclose their personal thoughts about a case in which they were presiding.

At the beginning of a civil case in 1957, the plaintiff was just being sworn in, when he told the usher he was an atheist. At this point, the judge, who was on the Bench and soon to be trying the case, was heard to say "and no morals either". The Court of Appeal set aside the verdict in that case and ordered a new trial as the judge had shown himself to have a bias against the plaintiff.

The most remarkable case of judicial slips appearing to prejudice the case was in an assault trial in London in 1968 before the Chairman of the Bench, Ewen Montagu QC, and a jury. Three men were convicted but appealed on the ground that the trial judge's conduct "vitiated the fairness of the trial" in that by "interruptions, grimaces, groans, sighs and exclamations of impatience" he had prejudiced the jury against the defence. Witnesses testified that at one point when defence counsel was cross-examining a prosecution witness, the judge observed in a loud voice "Oh God", and then "laid his head across his arm and made groaning noises". In a bizarre decision, the Court of Appeal disapproved of the judge's conduct but allowed the convictions to stand. It was then the turn of the defendants to exclaim "Oh God" and rest their heads on their arms.

A state of uncertainty

Vatican City is an independent sovereign city-state within the city of Rome. It covers an area of approximately 110 acres, and has a population of 800. The state is governed by the Pope with an administrative apparatus called the Roman Curia. It has a judge, a tribunal, an Appeals Court and a Supreme Court.

It would, therefore, have come as something of a surprise to the state in 2012 to find it was being sued in Russia by a man called Roman Lugovoi who asserted that he owned the Vatican. Russia's Supreme Court dismissed an appeal from Lugovoi who had litigated to claim legal dominion over the miniature state. The court was considering an appeal from Mr Lugovoi after his claim had been rejected in the lower courts. He had argued, with what he claimed was supporting documentation, that Vatican inheritance and property rights all belonged to him. He had sued the Pope personally.

This is not the first unusual large-scale legal claim brought by an individual in Russia. A Moscow arbitration court once dismissed a claim from a woman who had argued she owned a part of the Kremlin. She cited the then President, Dmitry Medvedev, the government, the Culture Ministry and the federal property agency Rosimushchestvo as defendants. She lost her claim.

The grandest claim to have gone through the Russian courts in recent history, however, was that of Marina Bai. In 2005, Russian lawyers litigated her case over activity at the final frontier: space. Ms Bai, a Russian astrologer, sued NASA for £165 million for "disrupting the balance of the universe". She claimed that the space agency's Deep Impact space probe, which was due to hit Comet Tempel 1 later that year to harvest material from the explosion, was a "terrorist act". She argued that the impact amounted to an assault on her grandparents as the comet heralded the beginning of their relationship. The sum of damages she sought was almost as much as the mission cost, and she claimed the right to compensation for her "moral sufferings". She stated that the comet had special significance for her family – when her grandparents met, her grandfather pointed out the comet to her future grandmother. NASA smashed an "impactor" (the size of a washing machine) into the comet to capture the debris released. Ms Bai argued that "It is obvious that elements of the comet's orbit and associated ephemera will change after the explosion, which interferes with my practice of astrology and deforms my horoscope". Her case was originally thrown out of a lower court on the ground that Russia had no jurisdiction over NASA, but the ruling was overturned when her lawyer was able to show that NASA's office in the US Embassy in Moscow does fall under Russian jurisdiction. Vladimir Fortov, a Russian physicist, said that the collision had no effect on the Earth and that "the change to the orbit of the comet after the collision was only about 10 cm". As the impactor collided with the comet when it was 82,642,368 miles away, the 10cm shift was not something the Russian court thought significant. Ms Bai's case was eventually rejected. Litigation, but not as we normally know it.

The hazard of Oz

The journalist Paul Bleakely said that the word "Australian" is a badge of honour, and one of the greatest compliments that can be paid to a person even if they are not from Australia.

A decision at Macclesfield Magistrates' Court in England in 2012, however, took a different view. The court convicted Petra Mills of a racially aggravated assault for calling her New Zealand neighbour "a stupid fat Australian bastard". Mrs Mills had called the police to her home following a domestic incident. At one point after they arrived, two police officers were questioning Mrs Mills' next door neighbour, Chelsea O'Reilly. Ms O'Reilly was from New Zealand but had a dual British-New Zealand citizenship. Ms O'Reilly was giving her statement to police about Mr and Mrs Mills when Mrs Mills raged across to her and began screaming at her on their street in Macclesfield, Cheshire. "She called me a stupid fat Australian bastard", Ms O'Reilly testified, "because of my accent there can be some confusion over my nationality. She knew I was New Zealand". "She was trying to be offensive", Ms O'Reilly said, "I was really insulted. She said she would kill my dog. Bizarrely she then blew raspberries at me like a child". Mrs Mills denied the charge. She testified that her outburst had been caused by the stress of moving house but denied it was racially motivated. "Yes I shouted at her", she said, "but it had nothing to do with racism". Mrs Mills' advocate said his client was angry at Ms O'Reilly's "snooping" and not her nationality. Mrs Mills said "I did not use the word Australian. I used to live with an Australian person. She was very nice". Both police officers, however, testified that Mills did use the word "Australian". Chairman of the Bench, Brian Donohue, said Mills was in "an emotional and inebriated state". He noted "The word Australian was used. It was racially aggravated and the main reason it was used was in hostility". Mills, who has since moved with her husband to Isle of Eriska in Scotland, admitted assaulting an officer by kicking him in the shin. She was fined £110 for racially aggravated public disorder and £200 for assault. She was ordered to pay her victims £50 compensation and £500 court costs.

In England and Wales, it is an offence to use "threatening, abusive or insulting words" within the earshot of someone likely to be caused harassment, alarm or distress. This has led to some controversial cases. In one 2006 incident, an Oxford University student was arrested after asking a mounted police officer if he realised his horse was gay. That charge, however, was later dropped.

The cleverest insults will always be those which are sharp enough to evade any law. When the flamboyant actress, Jean Harlow, kept mispronouncing Margot Asquith's first name, Asquith replied "the t is silent, as in Harlow".

The American author and wit, Dorothy Parker, was famous for her incisive ripostes. A younger playwright, Clare Boothe Luce, once paused by a door to let Parker go first, saying "age before beauty". Parker glided past, saying "pearls before swine".

The legally permissible level of insult to a lawyer in England was addressed in a case in 1639. Mr Justice Barckley observed that it was unacceptable to say of a lawyer that "he hath no more law than a monkey" but it was okay to say "he had as much law as a monkey". The second statement is merely an incomplete truth – lawyers *do* know as much law as monkeys plus a lot more. The colourful language lawyers later used privately against Mr Justice Barckley isn't recorded, but it is likely to have alarmed even the roughest troop of monkeys.

The Satanic Van defence

By common agreement, the Devil makes relatively few trips to Oxford.

He visited on one occasion, however, to cause trouble with sheep heads, according to Qasim Ali, a defendant at Oxford Magistrates' Court in 2013. Mr Ali was being prosecuted under the Environmental Protection Act 1990 for making an unauthorised waste deposit by the roadside. Among the bags which he had illegally fly-tipped was one containing a number of rotting sheep heads. Mr Ali, the manager of the Oxford Food Centre in Headington, claimed that he dumped the bags containing the sheep heads because "the devil had got inside of me". He said that while being driven in a van to a village in

Oxfordshire, the smell emanating from a bag in the van became so bad "I did not control myself". He said he felt impelled by an evil force to dump the bag. "Something just told me I had to get rid of the bag. The devil. I didn't know what was inside it. I felt something pushing me to do it and lost control of my body". The local authority was able to trace Mr Ali as the culprit because papers also found in the bag contained his personal details. Being demonically possessed, however, is not a defence recognised under the Environmental Protection Act 1990, so Mr Ali was found guilty and fined £750 for the fly tip, ordered to pay £500 prosecution costs, £200 clear-up costs and a £15 victim surcharge.

In a nominal way, the devil was used by lawyers. Historically, when the Roman Catholic Church was considering the canonisation of someone who lived an exemplary holy life, a canon lawyer known as the devil's advocate or *advocatus diaboli*, was appointed to argue against the canonisation. This process was designed to ensure that any weaknesses a candidate for sainthood might have were exposed in discussions. The official title, however, of the *advocatus diaboli* (literally, the devil's lawyer) was *fidei defensor* – defender of the faith.

Outside Oxford, the devil has been used in several defence arguments with varying degrees of success. In Malawi in 2004, a Catholic priest and a nun caught making love in the car park of Lilongwe airport had their sentences of six months' imprisonment with hard labour suspended after a plea of mitigation that they had been tempted by Satan.

In 2005, a prisoner in Romania identified in the law report as "Pavel M" sued God for having permitted the devil to win his soul. The plaintiff founded his claim in contract. He argued that his baptism was an agreement between him and God under which, in exchange for value like prayer, God would keep him out of trouble and beyond seduction by the devil. Lawyers for the prisoner, who is serving 20 years for murder, failed in their contention as they were unable to subpoena God to appear in the case.

In 1971, Gerald Mayo sued "Satan and His Staff" for violating his constitutional rights. His writ alleged that Satan had on numerous occasions "placed deliberate obstacles in plaintiff's path and caused his downfall". Judge Weber was very wary about allowing the action to proceed because so many people were arguably hindered by Satan and his staff that if Mr Mayo were to win, there could be an unmanageably large class action. The US District Court in Pennsylvania eventually dismissed the action for various reasons including that there was no evidence of Satan residing at an address within the jurisdiction of Pennsylvania.

The tooth, the whole tooth, and nothing but trouble

"My hand slipped" is an awkward excuse in law. Sometimes it might be plausible, such as where a person has entered the wrong date on a form, but it is always going to be more awkward if a dentist says that he pulled out 29 teeth from a patient in one sitting by mistake.

The story began when 21-year-old Christopher Crist went to Amazing Family Dental Care in Indianapolis, Indiana. By any account, what happened next was amazing, so at least the man doing the "dentistry" has that in his defence. In 2013 Mr Crist, who is autistic, explained to the dentist that his mother had said he needed to have three teeth removed. He was sedated. When he came to, he discovered that the three problematic teeth had been removed. So, however, had his other 29 teeth. He now had no teeth at all. Mr Crist was highly traumatised and told a local television channel "I am going to look like a freak now". After the original television report aired, other local residents came forward to report similar experiences at the hands of the dentist. Rose Hill said that she had been in shock after going to the same surgery about a single troublesome tooth and had undergone treatment in which the dentist removed her entire bottom row of teeth. A woman who was at the surgery when Mr Crist had his treatment said that when he came out, his mouth looked like "something out of a horror movie". Mr Crist's family said that he spent two days in hospital with a serious infection after the ordeal. Steve Eslinger, the lawyer for Amazing Family Dental Care, has issued a statement saying that his client, who has not made any comment, complies with the Health Insurance Portability and Accountability Act by keeping all patient information confidential and releasing it only to patients.

Bizarre dental practices have occasionally come to the attention of the law. One such case arose in 2008 and concerned the dental work of Alvaro Perez in Sampierdarena in northern Italy. Mr Perez, from Ecuador, was arrested after his patients reported that he had been knocking out their old fillings with screwdrivers and extracting teeth with household pliers. It transpired he had no qualifications in dentistry. His main apparatus was (please skip this next bit if you're of a sensitive disposition) a DIY power drill.

Another case of imperfect dental care involved Dr Alan Hutchinson, a dentist from Batley, West Yorkshire. He was struck off the register of practitioners for professional misconduct. The court found that Hutchinson had violated hygiene in several ways – including one occasion when a dental nurse caught him urinating in the dental sink and then treating a patient moments later without washing his hands.

Lawyers have had some amusement in cross-questioning dentists. One such story records the advocate who said to the worried dentist seated in the witness box "Now then, just sit back and try to relax, these questions won't hurt at all".

The award for best advocacy in a dental case, however, must go to Mr Justin Gau, in Wales. Mr Gau prosecuted Newton Johnson, a dentist in Llanelli, for defrauding the public purse of £37,555 for dental work he hadn't carried out. With his wife, the practice manager, Johnson had invented 100 patients including Varlo Johnson. As a false patient, Varlo was key to the case but wasn't very helpful in giving evidence because he was a Hungarian Wirehaired Vizsla, and was able only to bark. At the trial, Mr Gau used the context of the case to inspire some jaw-dropping phrasing. He told the court, "The fillings they performed were the fillings of their own wallets", and then noted that "They were saying to the public purse 'open wide' and performing a series of illegal extractions".

Courting disorder

In a case involving a litigant acting for herself in Queensland, Australia in 2013, the Court of Appeal faced an accusation that it was an unlawful court. Understandably, the judges were perplexed about why a litigant was keen to have her case judged by a court that she was arguing was incompetent to make rulings.

Lille Kosteska brought an appeal under the name "Lille: of the Kosteska family (as commonly known)" and also on behalf of "the Queen". The action was brought with a fairly wide compass of legal attack to correct "serious defects in the manner in which legal affairs especially of the nation generally ... are presently conducted, and have been for a very long time". Ms Kosteska is not a newcomer to the Australian courts. The case report notes she has been bringing actions "for many years". The latest action arose from various decisions made against her in the Cleveland Magistrates' Court in Brisbane. Ms Kosteska argued that the magistrate and the registrar of the State Penalties Enforcement Registry acted unfairly and unconstitutionally when trying to punish her. Since 2003, Ms Kosteska has been fined 36 times for offences including a variety of driving offences, a drugs offence, and possessing property suspected of being stolen. She owes US$15,278.60 to the courts and claims, in essence, that the law was not entitled to fine her as the legal system is illegitimate. Her action for judicial review of these decisions was rejected by a lower court so she applied to the Court of Appeal for permission to appeal. Ms Kosteska's legal claim was couched in an unusual style. In his leading judgment, Justice Martin noted that it "resembles the stream of consciousness style of writing used (more entertainingly) by authors such as Jack Kerouac". Using an array of precedents plus excerpts from books such as *A History of Money* and *The Second Treatise of Civil Government*, Ms Kosteska argued that the Australian legal system was supposed to deal with injustice but was "not up to that task". At her previous convictions, the trial judge had been supposed to abide by the ethos represented by the "British Coat of Arms" suspended above the Bench, she alleged, but the magistrate had failed to apply "the common law of England". Justice Martin rejected that point as a "truly sublime absurdity". Ms Kosteska also argued that "since at least 3 March 1986 at 5.00 GMT" when the Australia Act was passed by "the Imperial Parliament at Westminster", all laws purporting to be in force in Australia were invalid. If true, of course, that would have put Australian judges and lawyers in a position of considerable difficulty – they would be farmers in a desert. The Court of Appeal dismissed the case of "Lille: of the Kosteska family (as commonly known)". Although HRH the Queen was joined as a co-applicant by Lille, it is not yet clear whether Her Majesty was disappointed by the outcome of the case.

Litigants without lawyers have challenged the Australian courts in earlier cases. In his opening speech in the High Court in Canberra in 2003, Theodore Rout stretched philosophy to tearing point by saying that, along with the entire Australian legal system, he was a victim of "mythological peer review organisation that does not exist and is staffed by volunteer workers of which there are none". The court listened to a speech full of assertions such as "if everything is on nothing and you multiply it by zero, then the entire universe and the world does not exist. I have proven it conclusively". Mr Rout's case was dismissed because the court could not make any connection between his recondite reasoning in physics, and the litigation in question: an action to challenge the result of an election in the constituency of Fraser.

Fortune telling

Referring to the idea that "the meek shall inherit the earth" the lawyer, FE Smith, said "I have never found any particular corroboration of this aphorism in the records of Somerset House". Certainly, some wealthy people are not shy to use the courts to protect their reputations.

In 2013, Prince Alwaleed bin Talal of Saudi Arabia began litigation in London against *Forbes* magazine, saying it defamed him by calculating his wealth in a way that listed him with only US$20 billion. In reality, he argued, he had US$30 billion. When wealth is measured in billions, it can be difficult to conceptualise what that means. It is helpful to remember, however, that whereas a million seconds is 11 days, a billion seconds is 31 years. Under English defamation law, the tort of libel is committed if someone makes a statement which "tends to lower a person in the estimation of right thinking members of society generally or to cause him to be shunned or avoided". The wrong is also committed if the statement exposes a person to "hatred, contempt or ridicule", or disparages him "in his office, profession, calling, trade or business". How far the prince was lowered in public esteem or whether he was shunned by people for owning only US$20 billion remained to be seen. The prince said the magazine published a deliberately "insulting and inaccurate" picture of his business community and denigrated his country's stock exchange, the Tadawul. There are 1,426 billionaires on the *Forbes* "Rich List", and Prince Alwaleed was currently ranked 26th. His legal action related to the way in which *Forbes* calculated his wealth and to what it said in an article published alongside the list of wealthy people. He said his wealth was underestimated by US$9.6 billion. He stated that his legal action was not motivated by his ranked position itself but by the way *Forbes* cast aspersions on him by doubting the nature of his wealth. If the method he suggested should be used to calculate his wealth were to be used, he would be placed ninth in the Rich List. The prince argued that *Forbes* was using a "deeply flawed valuation methodology". The magazine defended its methods and stated that it has been subject to 25 years of "intermittent lobbying, cajoling and threatening" from the prince in relation to ranking on the billionaires list.

Along with businessmen, lawyers have used the law of defamation in some unusual cases. In a case in Scotland in 1781, a paper had published an article referring to the Worshipful Society of Solicitors as the "Worshipful

Society of Chaldeans [magicians], Cadies [errand boys] or Running-Stationers". The Worshipful Society of Solicitors then issued a writ faster than you can say abracadabra. James Boswell represented the paper's editor, and Dr Johnson wrote the defence for him, but they didn't do very well. Boswell argued that the paper should not pay damages to the solicitors because the mischievous reference had not resulted in them losing any fees. Turning to the alleged injured reputation of solicitors and whether it could be hurt by a slur, he asked, rather mercilessly, "what is their reputation but an instrument of getting money?" That line wasn't well received. The paper was found liable for defamation, and its editor was ordered to pay £5 damages and £15 costs. There are some places in society where insulting lawyers goes down very well but a law court isn't among them.

Toraburu ahead

The law is used to control language in many ways. It controls obscenity, defamation and perjury.

In Japan, a man sued the national public television channel for allegedly polluting the national language with too many English words. Hoji Takahashi sought 1.4 million yen (£9,300) in damages from the broadcaster NHK in 2013. His lawyer said that "the basis of his concern is that Japan is being too Americanised". After the Second World War, and during the US-led occupation, English words fell into local usage in Japan and their adoption has increased significantly in recent years. Japanese vocabulary now contains many words which have been adapted from English to fit with traditional phonic structures in which sounds are usually made of a consonant and a vowel. Mr Takahashi exemplified his legal claim with such words as "toraburu" (trouble), "risuku" (risk) and "shisutemu" (system), which feature commonly in NHK's news and entertainment programmes. He argued that the state broadcaster had a legal obligation to promote the culture of Japan and to protect Japanese from the linguistic impurities of other tongues. Other quasi-English words often used in Japanese include: pasokon (personal computer), terebi (TV), rajio (radio) and dejitaru (digital).

Similar concerns to those of Mr Takahashi in Japan were expressed in England in the 18th century where there was a strong feeling that too much Latin was being used in the law courts. So strong was the resentment, that an Act was passed by Parliament in 1731 abolishing Latin in legal proceedings. The Act lamented the use of an "unknown language" in the courts of justice as participants in the proceedings had "no knowledge or understanding of what is alleged for or against them". So the Act proclaimed that from then on, all writs, pleadings, indictments, and judgments "shall be in the English tongue and language only". Lawyers then faced the challenge of rendering all their hundreds of Latin phrases into English, so *nisi prius* became "unless before", and *quaere impedit* became "wherefore he hinders", and so forth. But the lawyers' withdrawal symptoms were, evidently, too much to bear so, in 1733, another Act was passed, permitting the Latin addicts in court once again to thrust and parry in their old argot.

Other countries have exercised some control over the use of their language in a way Mr Takahashi in Japan might appreciate, although foreign vocabulary has not technically been outlawed. In France, the so-called Toubon law of 1994 mandates French as the language to be used in government publications, adverts, parts of the news media and all state-funded schools, but there's no legal action if someone uses a word like "weekend".

The absorption of foreign vocabulary into British English has been prodigious, making it the verbally richest language in the world. English currently includes a number of Japanese words such as haiku, origami and Bonsai. For centuries after 1066, kings of England were more French than English. Over 10,000 French words became English words in the three centuries following the Norman invasion. Much of the writing in the Year Books (1260–1535) – the earliest case reports on which English law is founded – is in a type of French developed by lawyers and known as "Law French". After a while, the French language became widely resented and the

Statute of Pleading 1362 attempted to re-Anglicise the language of law. The Act deplored French usage in the courts, saying that most English people didn't understand it, and were thus unable to defend their rights. This bold Francophobic law suffered from only one weakness: it was written entirely in French.

Chapter 10

Technology

In 1911, the British mathematician and philosopher, Alfred North Whitehead, noted that "Civilization advances by extending the number of important operations which we can perform without thinking of them". Certainly, many lawyers and judges in cases involving technology have stories which verify North's observation. People have ended up in an astonishing range of difficulties in the context of new technology. In the future, some historians of our age might find much evidence in the law reports to substantiate the view of Aldous Huxley in 1937 that "Technological progress has merely provided us with more efficient means for going backwards".

In the second book in the series, *More Weird Cases*, the dramas included the case of a Canadian lawyer who complained to a court "My whole brain is in there" when ordered by the judge to shut his Macbook, a Swedish case concerning a boy legally taken into care for "chronic computer addiction", and a man who sued the designers of an online fantasy world for having made him unable to cope with the real world after spending 20,000 hours in theirs.

In the last couple of years, technology has continued to confound and baffle people in ways which recall the observation of the American political philosopher, Thomas Sowell, in 1996, that "The march of science and technology does not imply growing intellectual complexity in the lives of most people. It often means the opposite". Here are some of the cases in which the participants might have wanted to press Ctrl-Alt-Del.

Facebook status: prosecuted

Although social network sites host widespread fun, they're also the platform for disputes which end up in court.

In Carlsbad, New Mexico in 2011, Benito Apolinar faced prosecution for assaulting his wife because she failed to click "Like" on his latest Facebook status. Apolinar, 36, who lived in Texas, had posted a comment on his Facebook page about the anniversary of his mother's death. He later noticed that his estranged wife, Dolores, wasn't one of the people who had clicked "Like" beside his comment to indicate their approval. When on a visit to her, he told her that he was very unhappy about her failure to like his comment, and, according to the criminal battery charge, assaulted her. In her formal statement, Dolores Apolinar told police her husband came to her home and an argument between the two resulted in him pulling her hair and punching her in the face. In his defence, Benito argues Dolores hit *herself* in the face then hit in him the eyebrow with her cellphone.

The "she hit herself in the face" defence hasn't had much success in the UK. James Allen, a 61-year-old deputy High Court judge, was given a suspended 12-month supervision order in June 2010 after hitting his wife three times during an argument. Allen claimed in his defence that his wife had punched herself on the side of her head out of frustration – a version of events she herself claimed was true – but a doctor said otherwise and Allen was later found guilty of common assault.

Unlike the diffuse nature of social networks such as Twitter, the tighter family and friendship on Facebook can raise tensions in many relationships. As a tweeter noted, "Twitter makes me want to have drinks with people I don't know but Facebook makes me want to throw drinks at people I do know".

Other behaviour involving spouses who step into the virtual world has resulted in legal action. In 2008 in

Cornwall, Amy Pollard broke off her relationship with her husband after she discovered "Dave Barmy", his avatar on Second Life, was having a relationship with "Modesty McDonnell", another avatar. David Pollard said that the conduct of his dashing, goatee-bearded, sharp suited, medallion-wearing avatar – who lived in a mountain chalet and owned a gunship helicopter – wasn't wrong. He said he was just "hanging out" on Second Life. But Mr Pollard's view didn't prevail as the lawyer his wife went to for a divorce was one from real life.

Fiercebook

In a letter to his secret lover, George Bernard Shaw wrote "the ideal love affair is one conducted by post". Whether the same principle applies to Facebook romance is another question.

Cheryl Gray, in answer to that question, would certainly answer "no". Ms Gray, from Michigan, sued a man for US$8,368.88 in 2011 for leading her on and breaking his word and her heart over a six-month Facebook relationship. In her legal claim, Ms Gray, a 50-year-old paralegal, stated that Wylie Iwan, a 35-year-old from Washington, misled her during an online relationship which began while they were playing "Mafia Wars" on Facebook. When the relationship ended, she threw the paralegal book at him, suing for misrepresentation, defamation of character, intentional infliction of emotional distress and promissory estoppel – where someone can be taken to court for going back on an undertaking made during a contract. As their Facebook relationship bloomed, the couple also texted each other, emailed and spoke on the phone. Ms Gray bought gifts, including a digital camera, for Mr Iwan. She eventually booked an airline ticket, a hotel in Seattle and a rental car to visit him in his home state. But a week before the planned trip he told her not to come because he had met another woman in a bar. Mr Iwan denied that his relationship with Ms Gray ever moved beyond simple friendship. He said he had never intended to lead her on. He said "We decided we wanted to meet each other. After that things started towards a relationship, and we started sharing more information". "For Valentine's Day, she said she wanted to tell me she loved me as a friend", he explained, "I told her I love her too. I was meaning it as a friend". He said she originally told him she was 42, and then admitted being older just before the scheduled meeting. Ms Gray stated that she was very upset. She said Iwan had used the words "I'm falling in love with you". But later, she said, he wrote spiteful and untrue things about her on his Facebook page. Before suing him, she started a Facebook site describing him as a predator. Ms Gray did not win the case; a judge at the Livonia District Court in Michigan dismissed it, ruling that the court had no personal jurisdiction over the defendant as he is an out-of-state resident. Ms Gray argued the case was within the Michigan jurisdiction because the personal relationship constituted "doing business in Michigan" but the court rejected that argument.

This isn't the first odd case to have been generated by romance on the internet. The internet has generated a new and rare problem for jurisdictions with fault-based divorce: who is to blame if both partners are simultaneously disloyal? This can happen if, while apart and using aliases, they get passionate with each other in a chat room unaware of with whom they are getting intimate.

Sana and Adnan Klaric from Bosnia began divorce proceedings in 2007 after discovering that their respective secret chat-room lovers were, in fact, each other. They had been pouring their hearts out about their marriage problems under the online names of Sweetie and Prince of Joy, but sweetie turned sour and joy fell to woe when they decided to meet and found themselves staring at each other.

Cash offers wanted for perfect counterfeit machine

Sometimes behaviour tells its own story, as when a person accused of being violent punches his accuser.

Someone who tries to get a good price for his counterfeiting machine, because he needs the cash, tells an odd tale, and that is the story which a law court in

Michigan heard. Trying to convince a pawn shop that your counterfeit machine is a really good one, and therefore something for which you should get a large sum of money, raises the awkward question of why you are not at home with the machine whirring. That was part of the downfall of Kenny "Boom" Smith, who faced a federal indictment in Detroit in 2012 for making and passing counterfeit money. Mr Smith's alleged crime involved all kinds of madness. The defendant walked into a pawn shop with counterfeit cash and tried to negotiate a good price for the machine that produced the notes. The pawn shop he chose, however, was "American Jewellery and Loan" at which a renowned US hit TV show "Hardcore Pawn" is filmed. Les Gold, the owner of the store, has seen some odd characters in his time and he dealt with Mr Smith in a measured way. Extraordinarily, Mr Smith also expressed interest in being on the TV show. Smith told Mr Gold he would bring his counterfeiting equipment to the store. A short time later, US Secret Service agents arrived. They had been tracking Smith since he had started passing his fake bills. Mr Gold recounted what Smith had told him and the federal agents discovered Smith's counterfeiting claims had been caught on the shop camera which records transactions for the show.

Counterfeiting money and royal signatures has always been a serious crime. An English statute of 1351, the Treason Act, classified coin counterfeiting as high treason and required the culprit to be executed.

One of the oddest forms of counterfeiting was committed by Yupeng Deng. In 2011, he was convicted for an unprecedented crime which involved, in effect, counterfeiting an entire US army unit. Deng established the "US Army/Military Special Forces Reserve Unit" (MSFR) in Southern California and opened a recruiting office in Los Angeles. He then recruited and trained Chinese immigrants, telling them that joining would improve their chances of gaining full US citizenship. The recruits were charged US$300–US$450 to enlist, and up to US$120 each time their membership required renewal. They were also allowed to pay extra fees to Deng to gain a higher military rank. Deng wore an auspicious military uniform and was titled "the Supreme Commander". Deng's military office in Temple City was decorated as a real army recruiting station, and had a large rug featuring a US Army seal. Recruits were trained using mock weapons and were drilled in public places. Deng was convicted of various offences, including counterfeiting an official government seal.

The worst attempt to use illegal tender occurred at the UEA Central Bank in Abu Dhabi in 2010. A man was arrested after trying to trick a bank official to give smaller change for two US bills. The 44-year-old man, AB, from Ivory Coast, said the bank teller could take a 30 per cent cut if she changed the notes. He handed the bills over the counter, and that was when his plan crashed. The teller saw that each bill was for US$1 million.

Self-contempt

In a case in 1838, Mr Justice Williams noted there were so many versions of contempt of court that they would be "endless to enumerate".

One particularly intriguing version was recorded in Michigan, where a judge punished himself for committing contempt in his own court. During a criminal case in Ionia County District Court in 2013, the prosecutor's closing argument was interrupted by a loud voice saying things such as "I can't understand you. Say something like 'Mom'". Uneasiness spread through the court and attention then focussed on Judge Raymond Voet whose new smartphone, it turned out, was the source of the impatient voice. The phone, which was in the judge's pocket, was trying to get him to give it voice commands for voice dialling. The judge initially tried in vain to stop the phone from asking him questions but he was used to using a Blackberry and wasn't familiar with the touchscreen controls. It seemed like the more he tried to silence the phone, the more insistent it became to get him to speak. The judge said that he must have inadvertently bumped it into action. The trouble was that a special court edict, on the wall, asserted that any disturbance in court caused by electronic devices of any kind would result in the owner being instantly cited for contempt and fined. Judge Voet, therefore, cited himself for contempt. He said "If I cannot live by the rules that I enforce, then I have no business enforcing these rules". He fined himself US$25. He did not ask himself for time to pay the fine and settled the debt in full later that day.

Uncontrolled electronic devices have posed challenges for the Bench in some earlier cases. Magistrate Hector Graham was on the Bench at Luton Magistrates' Court just before Christmas in 2000. A convicted man dejectedly stood before the Bench, head hung, about to be sentenced for a property crime when the courtroom suddenly rang out to the tune "Santa Claus is Coming to Town". Mr Graham pulled open his jacket and agitatedly began fumbling with his musical novelty Santa Claus tie. The convicted defendant looked on incredulously. The magistrate's tie then burst into "We Wish You a Merry Christmas" before stopping, at which point the defendant was jailed for four months.

There is also precedent for a judge sentencing himself. Francis Evans Cornish was appointed as a QC in Canada in 1857. He was then aged 26. He became Winnipeg's first elected Mayor in 1874, a status which allowed him to sit as a magistrate. In this capacity, he once had to try himself on a charge of being drunk in public. After carefully considering the evidence, Cornish convicted himself and fined himself US$5 with costs. Cornish was, however, a considerate and thorough magistrate disposed to consider all relevant matters, so he then stated for the record "Francis Evans Cornish, taking into consideration past good behaviour, your fine is remitted". Later that day he allegedly fined another man US$10 and when asked about the high fine, replied that it was to send out a message as the offence was becoming too common.

Grand theft voto

A student who tried to win a university election in California by stealing the identities of 745 of his fellow students won a place in jail for a year in 2013. Matthew Weaver, a third-year business student at Cal State San

Marcos, stole the identities of 745 of his fellow students and cast their votes for himself as president of the university student council. Sentencing him to a year in jail for the crimes of "wire fraud" identity theft, and unauthorised access to a computer, Judge Larry Burns noted that an attempt at a cover up by Weaver after he was caught had compounded his wrongs.

Weaver had used a Facebook page fraudulently to try to make it look as if named students had framed him. Evidence gathered by police after the crimes showed that the story began early in 2012 when Weaver made a PowerPoint presentation to some fraternity friends in which he proposed that he run for campus president and that four of his fraternity brothers run for other jobs on the student council. The presentation noted that the president's job gave an US$8,000 stipend and the other positions each got a US$7,000 stipend. A "keylogger" is a small electronic device which secretly records what keys are hit on a computer keyboard. When police investigated Weaver's computer they found that his computer searches had included such questions as "how to rig an election" and "jail time for keylogger". The prosecution explained that Weaver installed keyloggers on 19 university computers, snatched passwords from 745 students, and cast votes from the accounts of more than 630 of those victims. The plot came to light in March 2012, the final day of the four-day voting period, when university computer technicians noticed suspicious voting patterns on one of the college computers in Academic Hall 204. Police were called and found Weaver sitting at the computer.

After a short period in jail, Weaver and an accomplice created fake Facebook pages using the names of real students. They then posted fictitious conversations to make it seem as if those students had conspired to frame Weaver. The "conversations" on those pages were sent to local news media. Had they been believed, Weaver would have falsely incriminated entirely innocent people. The judge did not accept that rather optimistic plea of defence counsel that Weaver's conduct was simply something triggered by a "juvenile sense of push-back" against the existing student council. Referring to the deceitful

Facebook attempt to frame innocent people, the judge said "He is on fire for this crime and then he pours gasoline on it". Weaver was asked to pay the US$40,000 bill to correct the security breach for 730 students, effectively requiring a new system of details for everyone.

Universities have housed some odd legal cases of dishonesty. In 2008, Jerome Drean and Elnar Askerov were sentenced to nine months' imprisonment, suspended for two years, after Drean took £20,000 for posing as Askerov in exams. Both men pleaded guilty to "conspiracy to defraud" the University of York. Drean, who was a very clever banker, sat economics exams in Askerov's place. Drean used a false ID card bearing his own photo but Askerov's name. They were caught when a lecturer in the hall noticed that someone was preparing to sit the exam who wasn't on the course and that Askerov wasn't present.

Another unusual case was that of Paul Moss in 1976. Mr Moss was a civil engineering student at Liverpool University. He was accused of stealing "intangible property" in the form of confidential information from the civil engineering exam paper due to be sat the following month. After he had read the questions he returned the paper itself to the place from which he had swiped it. It was agreed by both sides that he didn't intend to steal the paper itself but merely to look at the questions. The court held that, for the purposes of the Theft Act 1968, confidential information did not amount to "property" and could not be stolen. Mr Moss won the legal battle but it was a Pyrrhic victory because the court condemned him as a cheat.

INDEX